BRIDGE OUT!

full speed ahead

Gary R Kirby

GENERAL DEDICATION:

To The Greening Generation,

    who have inherited our graying world

        to whom we leave the enormous challenge

            of returning nature to its primal green

                in the face of corporate and cultural greed

                    rushing forward at a lethal pace.

Somehow they, and we, must help

    transform our energy and material uses

        into a high clean tech that harmonizes

            with the grass and the trees

              the rivers and the seas

                and the air we breathe

                  If they fail, we fail

                    and much of life fails.

SPECIAL DEDICATION

To my Son Scott Kirby, The Riverwalker, who while I just write about it, is actually doing something about it—taking care of some of our rivers in the Pacific Northwest.

Long before I did, Scott caught fire at the insults done to our earth. He opened my eyes to the duplicity of people whose positions are to protect the environment, but who care less about the earth than their own greed and power.

Scott monitors the health of the streams and rivers which flow from the Coastal Mountains of Oregon into the Pacific and the Columbia. He tracks the salmon and steel head trout as they rush into the rivers, checks to see if they can mount the ladders, analyzes the health of the banks of the waters, watches the fish spawn, charts the number and location of the reeds where they deposit their eggs, makes sure there are pools in the streams for the fry and fingerlings to gather until they are big enough to swim to the sea, and he notes which ones return to spawn.

Scott read this manuscript and caught several serious blunders. More importantly, he has started his own notebook of reflections, attractively entitled: *Notes from the Spawning Ground.* We hope to read them one day.

We thank you Riverwalker, and others like you, because you work and wish and want and will keep our waters and earth clean.

SPECIAL THANKS

To my son Matt, who made me aware of the prison of my culture. Ten years ago he challenged me to show him a single thing in the room of our house in which we were sitting, that had not hurt the earth, either in its making or transporting.

I could not do it. In fact, I could not find a single thing in my entire house, including some stones I had picked up while walking, for I had either driven them home in a polluting car, or walked them home upon synthetic shoes.

This book is the attempt to solve that problem.

contents

The boat drifts calmly
Moonlight ripples the water
Dreamers sleep

Waterfall.

Forty yards away, wet death yawns

Father forgive the dreamers
They knew not what they did

The giant car hums smoothly
Headlights swallow the asphalt
Passengers doze in oblivion

Bridge Out

Forty yards or years away, steel death gapes

Father forgive the car's creators
They knew not what they did

Father easy on the passengers
Drugged and drowsy of what they do

Father damn the drivers
Full knowing where they go

Father damn us all if we don't find out.

author's disclaimer

This book is honest. I swear to that, and I am honest.

There. If I'm not lying, that's all you need to know. You do, however, have to figure out when I am being humorous, ironic, satirical, salacious, shallow, insulting, or unintentionally arrogant.

I played the game of being a scholar for six years, the dissertation of which now blocks the dust from a shelf at Northwestern. Compared to the knowledge of the scientists, historians, environmentalists, sociologists, political scientists, philosophers, and my kids, this book sucks—hey guys, I'm just a Johnny-green-come-lately English teacher with nothing better to do with my summer than vent. The venting is a stream of semi-consciousness (emphasis on the *semi*) with the faucet stuck open.

Though I have not put anything into this book, which I do not believe to be true, please check any fact in this book before going to the wall with it. I'm kinda lazy, and I don't have a bevy of beautiful research assistants to, well, vet my facts. But I did check all my uncertainties at least once, and I paid attention to the reputability of the source; but being lazy and not liking bibliographical documentation, I have not usually told you where I found it. Google anything you don't believe, like the first internal combustion car being a hydrogen car; and if you do check up on me, I'm kinda biased toward looking for researched, credentialed sites, like universities. Not that there aren't liars among us teachers, but most of us don't teach for the money and we are not influential enough to be paid to falsify a position.

Will someone please tempt me? And make it big. I want to find my breaking point.

Prolog

to know
to know the human constructs
and the cosmic bookends

to know how we got here
and where we are going

to hope
to hope we can change

to act
to act not only for food drink shelter and sex
but to act against custom and comfort
against the inertia of culture

to know, to hope, to act
or to drive full speed ahead
with the bridge out

I have hurt our earth. As my knowledge increases, I am still doing harm. It is easy to point my blaming finger at the giant grip of culture in which I am helpless, so why not succumb to its seductively comfortable grasp? A grasp I might escape, but will crush my children.

Yet how can I succumb when that same giant hand that holds me smashes down like a fist on my sleeping mother? I am in that fist; I am a part of that fist.

Escaping that clasp seems impossible. Even if I could slip under a crease in those huge fingers, and if I could shed my clothes and run from house and car, where would I run to? The woods are almost gone that once might have held a few escapees.

No, I can't run, and you can't either.

We are caught in culture.

If we were born in a brothel, a ghetto, a barrio, a shack or a slum, we could step out of it because there is a place to step to. But we can't leave our technological chemical culture because it covers the earth. Somehow, smothering in these seemingly soft folds of protection, we must open the massive fist from within and change its very nature.

That is the quest of this book. I reach out to you for help. Please hold my hand, pardon my outbursts, and steady my footsteps. We all walk this planet together.

How did we catch ourselves in our own grasp? We did most of it in the last few generations. Although civilization was long in the making, and our species had eaten up many of the forests of the world, suddenly, recently, the mechanized, chemical assault became rapidly global. Largely started by our grandparents, increased by our parents, the destruction has run amuck by us—much of which was done without thinking.

History will absolve our fathers and mothers, for they knew not what they did. Their world exploded under their probing hands into this technological marvel/monster that glistens and shines like the sirens of old, while our air and our water grow sick.

From this point forward, history will not absolve any of us, because we know what we do. But there are ways to wheel our massive cultural inertia around. When we leave this planet in guilt or innocence, what will be the state of the earth that we pass to our children? It will be their greatest challenge--to save their planet, to save its life, to save themselves.

You could call this book a generational cultural biography of the road taken, not chosen.

Our parents sped along this road, ignorant of the broken bridge ahead. They had fled the golden glow of farmutopia, entered the silver shadow of Pandora's Shop, and birthed us among her mechanical and electrical toys— and now we wander in this great white out, with an intellectual awareness of the problem, but with an apathetic blindness to the solution. And what do we pass onto our children who are our green hope?

While the above color-coded structure is hopefully chronologically clear (and analogically appealing!), don't let the style fool you--I promise a rollicking, ironic, sardonic, sarcastic, humorous ride with flashbacks and fast forwards that might spin out of control. Hang on...

I throw this book in your face!

I apologize for not properly throwing my gauntlet to the ground, but I wanted to shock—to shock myself out of my comfortable lethargy, and to shock you, along with me, so we can do something about our cultural trajectory. If you are still reading, you just might have the gumption (or the digestive system of a goat) to finish this book.

I can throw the book, because it is not the biblical stone that comes with conditions about who is allowed to cast it first. Certainly that wouldn't be me, for I am with environmental guilt--which would disqualify me from hurling anything. But I will hurl anyway--I will throw a lot of oaths at a lot of oafs, including myself.

I write for you, I write for our children. I write to crack this cultural bind that holds you, holds me. I write for our world.

If these struggling words work for you, I share them gladly. If they don't, please formulate your own; for if our words, or another's do not work soon, death by stoning would be a classy way to exit.

I lash out particularly at those who know and still destroy. To those people who are the cancers in our civilization, I have sharpened my words into caustic ridicule.

I also lash myself, (quite lightly, barely breaking the skin, I admit) to do what I now know I must do. I hurl at myself. I beat my head with my book trying to wake and shake myself out of a lethal lethargy, to coax, curse, cajole, and if I could, coerce myself into action to break free, to begin to heal, to begin to do what I know I should do.

And as I lash myself, I laugh. It hurts less that way. Laughter can heal as it cuts. And I am having fun in the writing, and I wish you so in the reading.

If you still hold this book, you have picked up the gauntlet. You must now read. Or be called a coward. And if I have angered you, please address all heated correspondence and suspicious packages to: Coward / Cobarde / Couard / Angsthase).

So as I throw this book in faces including my own, go ahead curse at and with me, laugh with me, and then begin the cure—to know, to hope, and then to do.

forward

Okay. So I already had my opening shot with the *Prolog.* What gives with a *Foreword*? I am quite chronologically correct, for *prolog* is of Greek/Latin origin and thus precedes *foreword* which is of Anglo/Saxon origin. So cut my double-dipping a break.

"Who's to bless and who's to blame?"

We'll answer that question in four generations—and most of us are in the last two of those generations.

But a more important question looms: into what hell (or heaven) are we hurtling? That hell is physically forming into clear, geological/cultural markers. Read the sign: *Bridge out, full speed ahead.*

And the most important question: can we turn this massive cultural machine around? And if we can, will we?

We had it.

We lost it.

Our days are not as good as the good old days. And yes, I know that most generations look back to their youth as the good days. So, probably they were never that good and they really weren't that old and far away either.

Not long ago we had it. Yet we lost it. We lost the touch of eden, the fresh earth when it blushed pine green in virginity below a pure blue sky. Sure, the sky still seems blue (if you are not looking horizontally from a distance into that slice of sickness that hangs over most of our cities). And the sky still seems clear at night (if you are not trying to count to 5,000, the approximate number of stars up to magnitude 6 which were once visible to your eyes, and many of which are now blotted by the thick offal in our air). And yes, the earth still seems green--witness the green monocrop of corn ringing the suburbs ringing the cities.

With stars winking out in the skies, and corn usurping flora in the fields, we are on a geometrically eroding progression.

Can we regain it?

No. Never like it was. But can we try to stop the erosion? Alone, we can't--like one person pushing against the giant car containing civilization, it would be useless. Alone we fight and die with a clean conscience but swatted like a fly on the windshield.

But together, maybe we can begin to slow the massive inertia of the huge wheels. Since our recent family line set this machine in motion, since we empower it now, theoretically we can slow it, stop it, or guide it. It is doable, but damnably difficult (my daughter hates my alliteration—so if you have her mindset, and I wouldn't mind having her mind, I apologize--I'm so seriously sorry for this sibilance).

Europe was the first to let the monster out of its coal mines and into their factories, from parlor looms into Cartwright's powered looms. America adopted the monster, fed its fire-bellied furnaces, gave it full legal rights, and then ran wild with it. As the greatest polluter per person, America must now lead the way out of the miasma, back into earth health. It is that--or die as a civilization. I say that not as an alarmist, but simply as a man who has lived and watched the earth change, who has seen the clear creeks of his youth buried under suburbs, who has stood on Montana's glaciers that are now gone, and who has read barely enough science and history to understand the recent impact on our old earth.

Science is the tool understanding the wings of the dove and the fangs of the snake; and it is in the hands of the father and mother monster which is in us all. We know how to use that same tool of science which has released the belching, ripping, tearing monsters turned loose on the planet, to tame those monsters--but we do not have the urgency, and therefore do not have the political will to do so.

The monsters lie not in science, nor in the giant machine caroming recklessly forward; the monsters lie in us, in our unreflecting, greedy selves.

Uh oh. That means changing something like a tooth extraction, dieting, or quitting smoking. Hard. But after dropping that hanging adipose, or breaking that chain of smoking, don't you feel better? A hard change can be a healthy change—and worth it.

So change. If not for yourself, then for your children--or for your favorite niece or nephew or some young person, who might be at your dying bedside, and who you hope will be gentle with you--and remember you for a while. For those people, if not for yourself, please change. Change first your own living style. Secondly, change your culture.

Apologies to your parents for not including them in this generational odyssey. Your fault. You didn't send me their stories, but I am sure you can read the paths of my fathers' as paralleling the lives of your parents and grandparents. To make sure it is relevant to you also, I will highlight our cultural points which show the speed, the steps, and the causes of our civilization crashing off course.

Apologies to the Kirbys for getting a lot of Dad's life wrong. I didn't ask Dad for his stories, and he did not brag or boast of his life. I know my brother Dave has different memories (but Dave is brighter than I, so please discount his recall).

Apologies to my children—I have used them mercilessly, and have passed an almost unbearable burden onto them.

Apologies to me, (I am CMA), for any mistakes I make. I have tried to be as accurate and honest as irony, sarcasm, anger, and pure fun at the fatal oddity of it all would allow. If you doubt something, google it. I don't cite all sources because this book would crawl like my dissertation.

Apologies to literati for rambling like Rabelais, for failing the pen of Voltaire while swearing like a sailor-- and therefore, apologies to my mother tongue. If you find all 103 non-sequiturs, I will give you a free book. While counting, do not include the sick segues because literary sickness, like beauty, is in the eye of the beholder: if you find a sick segue, suspect the source.

a moment in the present

This is my world. This is your world. This is my story. This is your story.

Buried so deep within us that we cannot touch them, unknown drives and forces from evolutionary time come burbling and floating, swimming and scuttling, crawling and climbing, and walking forth. We have stepped out of nature in the feet of our ancestors only a few short evolutionary seconds ago, and we changed the earth.

Most of that terraforming can be seen in the four parts of my story--and those same parts in your story. I think we have a few pangs of conscience and some huge healing we need to do. We will meet that challenge in The Great White Out. You can help me to write that part when we get there. In fact, like it or not, you must help me write that one. You'll understand later.

I tried to fictionalize our story for you, but I failed. Fiction has a way of letting the truth slip out: after all, *truth will out* was first uttered in fiction. I'm afraid this book holds far too challenging truth to slip it inside fiction. We have to look into the face of our culture and reject much of what we have accepted as true and good, the culture we grew up in it, comfy, fed, and fat. I certainly did, and the effort to turn my head around and see otherwise is Plato's challenge in his cave.

Can we find the real in our lives, in this book? The raw real? The blood dripping, rust-covered, brightest-smile-on-a-child's-face real. To find it in this book you have to double the hyperbole, sharpen the sarcasm, hypo-freeze the satire, and hype the humor by powers of ten. Laugh. Laugh with me. Laugh at me. And laugh at the Exxon Execs and Monsanto's monsters even as you curse them. You'll be happier that way, and your life-sentence will feel shorter.

I said I was afraid. Intellectually I fear; emotionally I hope. I choose emotions over reason--a rational choice. If that seems contradictory to you, it is. It is the paradox we live in.

We are crucified on this cross of contradiction, called civilization.

With our hands nailed we must break free. And biased though it may be, I choose the emotionally positive as I spin our story in the sucking maelstrom. (Am I now letting fiction slip into this truth?) I must choose the emotionally positive, for I must have hope in my story and hope in yours. You see, we read our past, and from it we choose to live or die.

Correction—we die whatsoever we choose. All do. But how will we die? That is the question.

And how do we feel about ourselves when we go screaming or smiling above the pain and fear of passing into the unknowing? That too is the question.

And how soon? Another question.

And whom do we drag with us? Our children?

But screw this dying stuff—the bigger question is: How do we live? And what do we leave behind?

Okay, two questions in one, but so related in cause and effect that we can call them one. After all, how we live is what we leave behind.

And Shakespeare notwithstanding--that is the question.

How do we live, and what do we leave? That question, the answer of which is the worth of our lives, can be rephrased in several ways. What will happen to our children sixty yards down the road? And our grandchildren? Born and unborn? And will they ever drive on civilization's roads that are constricting the earth? And if so, for how long and how far?

Not very far, according to the huge lines of force pushing us towards an overwhelming conclusion; but maybe they will get some distance out of their lives if we join together, as humans have rarely done before, and bend those huge lines—then we can write a different ending.

Later for the bending. First our titular metaphor of civilization's car going full speed ahead, even though the drivers see the sign: *Bridge Out*. I love metaphors! I have already assaulted your analogical sense with a fist, a cross, a monster, and this new analogy is not quite Steinbeck's turtle nor Route 66, but it's got a bit more motion than both of them, and it's hurtling towards stone and steel, and it has us in it. And maybe we are more than metaphorically in it.

I took a camping trip that pushed us perilously closer to that broken bridge. Motoring along in my huge van, I have pumped 5.5 x 3.7 x 175 pounds of pollution into your air on a single trip. That's 3,561 pounds of carbon dioxide!

(If you don't want the math, skip this parenthetical paragraph, and trust me. 5.5 pounds is the weight of carbon in a gallon of gas. When carbon burns and yields carbon dioxide, it becomes 3.7 times heavier. The carbon atom has an atomic weight of 12, and the two oxygen atoms weigh 16 each, yielding $12 + 16 + 16 = 44$; so an atom of carbon goes from a weight of 12 to a weight of 44 or increases 3.7 times. 175 is the number of gallons of gas I burned. (Add your own gallons you burn into this formula to calculate your own driving weight that you hang upon the world).

I'm a show-off. I could have just told you that if you get about 20 miles to the gallon, you put about a pound of CO_2 into the air for each mile you drive!

Driving so much makes me an itinerant criminal and sinner. In a ritualistic Catholic confessional formula that I said as a kid: *Bless me Father, for I have sinned exceedingly in thought, word and in deed* And indeed I knew what I had done. Yes, in just a week and a half I confess to having polluted the air you breathe by dumping 1 ¾ tons, yes tons, on a trip from Wisconsin to the Rockies. I write this confession out of a great guilt with a little hope. I knew it, and I did it anyway. Therefore I have no right to write this book, no, not even in fiction form because *Father I have sinned, and Father, you might not forgive me, for I knew what I would do.*

And I did it.

And right now you are sitting with me in the Grand Civil Supreme Sedan that carries us humans and all our making towards the bridge out ahead. Enjoy the ride. The end won't be pleasant, but the company is good—me.

And as you sit with me, your weight too is breaking this world. Perhaps you know it better than I. Or perhaps you motor along, obliviously guiltless. Drive on in peace, and I won't blame you. How can I? Did I not just confess to almost two tons of guilt? And beware the rest of our biography, because guilt comes with knowledge, and guilt preys grey and dark upon the mind.

But what do we do with the guilt? Notice how I have not mentioned global warming, and I might not for the rest of this book, so you can enjoy it while you subconsciously beat yourself for guilt). Fortunately, Freud has taught us how to rationalize. I do it all the time.

So let's rationalize.

Rationalization Number One: CO_2. It's natural. It's in our lungs and we breathe it out. What's the big deal?

Hold it. Just why do you think we exhale it? What if your lungs were full of only CO_2? The answer is obvious. Death. If you want to watch what happens when a large cloud of CO_2 descends over people and animals, just google *Lake Nyos*. Where are the villagers of Nyos? And of Subum? Of Cha? Of Kam? From the cadence of the rhetorical question reminiscent of *where are the snows of yesteryear*, I'm sure you know the answer. They are all dead. Over 1700 people dead from CO_2 released into the air. Not nice stuff. So just ignore the global climate change, which I'm not mentioning, and think of thickening the amount of CO_2 in the air. Ah…! Breathe deeply.

Uh oh. Let's skip that counter rationalizing process of logic and facts. Back to the good old mind-blinding rationalizations.

Rationalization Number Two: On my trip I had three (3) passengers. Count them: my wife, my son, and me. Now I can share with three people and spread that thick, smelly (okay, maybe it is odorless, but cut me a break—after all we are struggling with linguistic reality here, and the fictional reality or the real fiction of our lives calls for some forgiveness; and besides, it is thick, it is heavier than air)—as I was saying before you challenged the word, *smelly*, I can now spread 3,561 pounds of pollution over the souls of three people. Presto, I have vanished a third of my guilt and have only polluted 1,187 pounds.

Rationalization Number Three: Since the trip took ten days, I was really only polluting 119 pounds per day, less than my body weight. (Ugly image—who would want to breathe the disintegrating atoms of my body tossed into the air as pollution once a day. But wait a minute—I am supposed to be alleviating, not burdening my conscience. On with the rationalizing task at hand). As you see, dividing by 3 and then by 10 I have only 3% of my guilt left.

Rationalization Number Four: The reason I was taking the trip in the first place was to camp in the mountains, and thus appreciate the natural world even more and thus be more sensitive as to how I treat our world and thus be able to write our mutual biography and forthcoming obit with greater force. How much of the 3% does that decrease?

Rationalization Number Five: Another son met us camping. Family bonding! And don't ask about his polluting transportation allotments to join us. Nor about our campfires.

And this hard logic or loose rationalization is important. Have you ever cancelled or curtailed a vacation to be more gentle on the environment?

And don't ask about that stolen rock I tried to bring home. The rock was missing when I searched the old van. My purist son, who picks up litter when he sees it, told me that I had no moral ecological right to take that rock. He probably opened the van, took out the rock and returned it to its rightful place on the planet. In that rock, in that son, in our children lies our Green Hope, our last chapter. Can we at least help our green children help our world?

So surely these rational rationalizations, especially the appreciation of nature and parent/child bonding, are sufficient to rationalize away my mere 3%. Counter logic be damned! Do not ask what would happen to our planet if 8 billion people put their own 119 pounds a day up there like I did. Almost a trillion pounds a day! I wonder how much more that thin precious air of life that blows above us can hold? Oh well, I did my part rationalizing. And you, when this biography wanders too far from your life style, please do your own rationalization. For instance, if you did not have two passengers with you to spread the guilt, just say that at least you weren't driving an old gas guzzling

Hummer, (but maybe a Yukon or Escalade?) and then do the math difference. And think of all the pollution you saved!

But if you were driving a Hummer you could swab your guilty brain with a gasoline solvent, and then compare your savings to that of driving a tank--which gets about a third of a mile to the gallon. But if you actually drive a Hummer, then the hell with you. You just don't give a damn, and no rationalization will work with you, no, not even that one about protecting your kids in the Hummer from the predator Prius. Hummer drivers, get the hell out of our biography. If you are still in, you probably have choked on this book by now anyway.

But again, who am I without sin to cast the first pound of CO_2 into the air as I drive my Hummer-like Van?

I know the bridge is out, because I live in this intellectual generation of the Great White Out, I can read the sign.

But time to get on with the story by stepping back into the golden glow of a harvest in South Carolina.

the golden glow

The boat drifts calmly,
moonlight ripples the water,
dreamers sleep.
Waterfall!

Father forgive the dreamers,
for they knew not what they did.

How did we lose the farm?

How did that golden corn and waving wheat ever
fade? Could no one back then see the creeping shadow of
the coming combine? Could no one feel the shaking ground
from a disturbing, distant rumbling?

That time on the farm, less than 150 years ago,
wasn't really that golden. No age ever was. Olden times
seen through old eyes look golden. Such is the softening
power of memory. But compared to the current air we
breathe, the water we drink, and the ground we stand on
now, those days not long ago were indeed golden. Ask the
earth.

You are the point of a pyramid, and like it or not, your forefather was a farmer. Just like my Dad. (Okay, a few of you had hunters and gatherers even after 12000 BCE.) Your farming ancestors have stood with me and mine on the farm, or in the factory, or in the great white-out, or even on all three of those giant steps. And don't give me that stuff like my wife does, that she was descended from the Lord Chamberlain to William the Conqueror. Lord Chamberlain, whosoever he is, also grew up on a farm, whether he called it a manor or not. And if you do selective genealogy, you'll find that your Lord Chamberlain equivalent, back in 1066 or so, was also a farmer. In fact almost all of our forefathers were farmers—okay, toss in a few Daniel Boones.

Let's call a generation 25 years—don't fight me on this; I know Methuselah lived 969 years, but he was closer to the cleaner environment of the genesis garden of eden, so he lived longer. If you go along with the rounded-off math, every hundred years there are four generations, and going back nine hundred years or so to my wife's revered ancestor, that makes 36 generations (4 x 9 = 36). Now here comes the hard part: each one of us has two parents, four grandparents, and so forth, so $2^{36} = 137,438,953,472$. Got it? That math is infallible. And we would not be here without each one of those ancestors. So when William the Conqueror was bastardizing French down the English throats, my wife had 137 billion farmer ancestors!

Now don't tell me the population of the earth is less than 8 billion now, and don't tell me that back in woods of the dragon days of St. George the population was a bit thinner. That number stands: 137 billion. But I said this book was not a work of fiction, so now, what gives?

The answer is incest. And a pyramid that is really a diamond. That diamond, of which you are the living point, is still narrow and sharp when it opens to two at your parents, but it gets pretty fat back around the twentieth generation where it is slightly above 2 million, and then it begins to narrow into the shape of a diamond, as it gets closer to my wife's Lord Chamberlain.

Yep. That means lots of incest going on back then—well, at least a lot of distant cousins sleeping with other cousins. It had to be. Somewhere there were a whole lot of farmers sleeping in that wonderfully warm and musky diamond haystack that made you.

So your forefather was a farmer. No sweat. His land, his golden time was farmutopia. And he lived only a few generations back. Farmutopia was utopia for the earth, back in my granddad's day.

So how did we get from the farm to here, and who crapped up the world so fast? All this pollution guilt can't be ours alone, so let's see if we can pitchfork some of it backwards. And we won't have to dig too deeply into our roots (slight metaphor shift here, but not quite the horrendous-to-be-avoided-mixed metaphor) to see the beginning of the root rot. In fact, the rot grows grievously close to our toes. Sorry, you might not like that metaphor either, and since I'm talking about my Dad's line here (oops, and mine) I don't either.

I loved my Dad, and when he died, a lot of his goodness went into the soil, and I hope he left a little bit in me.

My Dad was born on a farm. A small, five-acre plot in Gaffney, South Carolina not far from the Blue Ridge Mountains where there is still a touch of that pine green virginity, close to where the Blue Ridge can wave to the Appalachians and onto the Great Smoky Mountains. I don't know much about Dad's Dad who died the year I was born. Dad wasn't much of a talker, nor I a listener.

And your Dad's Dad was also born on a farm. Okay, I might be a little older than you, but quit correcting me about your nomadic or arboreal royal ancestors and write your own book—but only after you read this one. Since this story is yours too, you could rightfully complain that farms really started about 12 thousand years ago, and therefore we ought to start our story then. Okay smarty, but what can we say about our direct ancestors way back then? I challenge you to name one of them--and don't use the-we're-all-connected-by-math which I just did.

Since our known genealogy is not quite 12 millennia deep, I think we can telescope our story about the farm into our more immediate ancestors. After all, a short time before them, farms were pre-chemical and pre-mechanized. That's an important difference. Farms were still small and fresh, and far, far less harmful. Soil was broken by wooden plows before Jethro Wood, ironically named, made the first iron plow in 1820. No smoking monsters were ripping the farm.

How harmful were those earlier, smoke free contraptions pulled by teams of oxen and horses? More furrows faster, much more food, still little damage, still pre-industrialized, pre-chemical farms for the most part. Still fresh, almost as fresh as 12,000 years ago.

Granted that farmers had been de-foresting and destroying natural vegetation since their inception, and granted that farms increased the food which increased the people into a population problem, let's just presume that by all comparative standards with the corporate conglomerates of Cargill, Monsanto, and ADM, the early farms were much, much closer to the natural world.

If you wish to press the point of our earthly destruction before the industrial revolution, then why not pass our earth changing guilt onto the first terraforming monkey who jammed a stick down a termite hole?

Don't laugh. You can't shake off your guilt by this moment of absurdity here. But then, maybe it's not so absurd. What was the origin of this terraforming devil monkey? Maybe that question is philosophically, theologically, teleologically, anthropologically, and primatologically sound. What if we blame nature for the whole thing? After all nature produced us, the terraforming ape.

No. Don't do that. You've gone too far and too deep. That's like blaming the earthquake on the star that burst and formed our solar system.

So. Let's get back to recent farms. In 1868, when my great grandfather Frank Davis Kirby was 13, the first steam tractor sputtered and bellowed and started pulling some logs around. The earth shuddered. I know it did. I can feel it in my genetic bones. Then in 1892 the gas tractor was unleashed on a farm field in South Dakota. And the earth shook. I really don't know the spot of that first mechanized, brutalized field, but it was in that state with the Badlands. I'm convinced that the *Bad-lands* were the punishment for releasing fire-breathing monsters upon the earth--reminiscent of the Promethean legend?

Now don't get me wrong. I don't hate machines. And I certainly don't hate farms. My Dad was born and grew up on a farm. And even though I learned about farms by singing *Old MacDonald*, I've always had a nostalgic childhood wish to have been raised on one. I did visit a few farms as a kid. To me then, cows and chickens and horses and pigs were the real thing. They held a mystery of naturalness, and I absorbed them wide-eyed. They didn't posture or primp or act artificially nice. They just were. They were just themselves, awesome living beasts that were tamed. And I still treasure farms. And, in a way, I am returning to them. Especially to those who cultivate wisely with nature. After all, like you, I love to eat. In fact, I created an acronym that I will share with you that would solve some of the problems: L O V E: eat Local, Organic, and more Vegetables and that will be better for the Earth. And you will be healthier, and if she could, the Earth would love you right back.

Now in 1892 when that first gas burning tractor was spewing and ripping and tearing up South Dakota, my grandfather, Thomas Worth Kirby, was a strapping youth of 18. (What the hell does *strapping* mean? Time for a digression here: my Dad said "strapping", and I think it meant tall and strong as he described his father Thomas as 6'2," a man who could pick him and his brother up in each hand like he was curling weights. But I also looked *strapper* up in *The Oxford English Dictionary,* the best ever written. There are an amazing number of meanings for *strapper*! You will have to check them all out yourself on page 1085, but I will share with you that the word was first applied to a tall goddess and then migrated to women who were large and amply rounded: Tobias Smollett has his hero, Pickle, pay a compliment a woman: "Ah. You strapper, what a jolly bitch you are!"

But his strapping size and sex are not the issue--his age was. When he was 17 there were no gas tractors chugging around the fields of South Carolina, or anywhere else in the country for that matter. Think of it—only a few generations back, and no oil-powered farm machines anywhere. No bulldozers plowing down any trees.

How fast we have stripped nature of her clothes and shrouded the land in farm fields.

Most of our terra-deforming has occurred recently, because before mechanization, farm fields were relatively stable and small. Sure, those farms too stamped their own damage on the earth, dug up natural vegetation, overworked the soil with single crops, depleted certain nutrients, allowed for insect hordes, and irrigated in disregard for natural water systems. But with all those terra-deforming changes, those early farms still looked closer to nature in her birthday suit. Closer to the earth our great grandparents walked upon.

But now there's poison in them there fields! In 1873 arsenic was first sprayed on crops, and in the very next year

DDT was concocted. I know my great granddaddy didn't have to deal with any of that. And at least at his birth, my grandfather never had the opportunity to breathe any DDT. (I did. Much later as a kid when a neat smell was added to DDT, I might have killed a little part of me along with the many flies I shot down on the wing.)

And the pre-industrial forests were green and huge, at least over a lot of our country. If you drive to the Pacific Coast on the Sunset Highway through Oregon, you will notice a thin curtain of cosmetic trees along the road; but behind them, clear-cut, stump scarred land. These clear cuts were recent, Weyerhaeuser cut and ran and sold their land. On this same highway, if you stop at Camp Eighteen you will see a glorification of the lumber industry. If you look closely at the displays, you will see that even their biggest hand saws could not take the once giant trees down. And they did not even try to cut them, because they could not transport them. Enter the mechanized steam donkey. It sputtered and roared and dragged the largest logs out. The old growth trees, giants of more than a thousand years, fell and are gone.

Like the land and the forest, the air was pure only a short time ago. (Don't be a purist and tell me humans were polluting the air with carbon from their fires, discovered about a million years ago, give or take a million years.) Before that...ahhh...clear nitrogen, oxygen, and less than 1% of argon, CO_2 (before my two ton contribution), neon, helium (heh, heh), methane (excuse me), krypton—let's stop with krypton--the world needs a Superman, and I'm afraid you, my readers, are going to have to replace him to save the world. Not me. I took the big van on the two-ton trip.

Breathe! Only pure air and some wind borne particles back then--nothing else! Air! Our granddads could wake in the morning and inhale pure air as a welcoming gift from nature. They breathed none of the 189 toxic airborne chemicals on an old list of the EPA, and there are really a lot more toxins, since many chemicals on that list are entire groups of chemicals and the list is growing. You and I are breathing the poisons right now.

Our ancestors are our heritage, but are they also our destiny? We have been imprinted, impacted, and formed. By looking briefly backwards (Bellamy be thanked) maybe we can scan further forwards, maybe further than twenty, or thirty, or forty yards or years away. Maybe, just maybe, if we all hang together and pull, maybe we can begin to turn that massive steering wheel of Civil Supreme, that gigantic speeding car manufactured by a consortium of the whole world.

Bridge Out Ahead!

Can we hang guilt on our grandparents? Probably not, even though pesticides were beginning to sprinkle the earth and tractors to rip into it; from their point of view, that was progress. Why not kill the bugs that ate their crops? And if you could plow a field in a day that took you three weeks before, why not? Of course they would. And they did. And we applaud them. For none of them had read *The Silent Spring;* and *An Inconvenient Truth* was not only inconvenient, but it was unknown. No knowledge, no guilt.

Who then was the prophet crying in the dying wilderness?

But now with hindsight, how can we be blind? Do we act much differently? That's partly why I'm digging and writing— to understand my own guilt, and to understand this toxic cross of civilization which our fore parents and we have raised. And to which I am nailed. And you are nailed, maybe without your knowing it. And who drove those nails? And who cut those giant cross timbers? And who joined them? And what powers erected that structure so toweringly high, casting its shadow darkening the Bridge Out and all life on earth?

And how the hell do we come down from it?

Will it fall, leaning, tottering, and rotting slowly at its base? Will we weaken, grow anemic, our blood dripping from the top? Or perhaps more likely--a sudden, thunderous crash sooner than we expect? Or project? Or even care to think about?

Disasters are like that.

Grandfathers, we forgive you, for you knew not what you did when you helped Pandora open her silver shop.

the silver shadow

The giant car hums smoothly,
 Headlights swallow the asphalt interstate
The passengers rock into oblivion.

Bridge Out!

Father forgive the dreamers, for they knew not what
they did.
Father partially forgive the drivers, semi-conscious
of what they do.

Softly the silver undulating shadow, swaying amidst
steel and smoke, entranced the young boy.
He fled the farm for Pandora's Shop, seduced by her
glittering power.
He ran full tilt into our mechanized society:
projectionist at 10, new car owner at 12, train jumper at 13,
tunnel blaster at 18, plane builder at 20, millwright for the
war machine, and finally and more happily, carpenter
shaping the softer world of wood—but Pandora's buzz saw
still screamed in the basement.

He was 10 when Pandora came to his farm, reached out her soft hand, and took him to the movies, to the silent silver screen, to the Star Theatre in Gaffney, South Carolina. Mesmerized, he drove out of her flickering shop in a new Dodge that he bought when he was 12. He crashed and rolled. So Pandora handed him, gift wrapped in straw, dynamite with which he blasted tunnels through mountains. She took his hands and danced, dominatingly, whirling his feet off the ground and into the sky as she taught him how to build his own airplane. She took him up, up on a spinning ride more dizzy and crazed than any drug induced hallucination. Because it was real. It was bird flight. And far below, her shops heaved mighty ships, stern first down her birthing canal into the sea, steaming him off to China and the opium dens--and then, in final, full seduction, she drew him into her bedroom--her factory, the lure of so many strapping farmers, where my father tended her machines to feed the battle hunger of Mars. Somehow Dad escaped from her factory, back into a partially healing world of wood. He worked in his own basement shop, but which still held a piece of Zeus's lightning crackling in his buzz saw.

I will explain those cryptic images of my father; perhaps they will help you and me to know where we came from and how we got here. And where we are going.

Dad, forgive me, for letting your images flicker before the world, Dad forgive me, for using you, mechanizing you. Dad, I am selecting only the parts of your life that help me to understand that we are hurtling inside of Grand Civil Supreme. Only a century before your birth, Gaffney was nothing but the crossing of two Indian trails. Now all paths and rivers and roads flow together onto the same Industrial Technological Highway, leading toward the same ending point.

And only two years before you were born poor, (poor being defined as seven kids on a five-acre farm) a bicycle chain turned a fan blade powered by a gasoline engine hooked to some bird wings that got airborne at Kitty Hawk. Dad would shortly challenge those clouds, joining that race ever faster and higher, by building his own plane.

But Dad's fledgling flight was indoors in the form of a movie projector. Pandora drew the boy close, too close to resist the perfume of the new, of the shiny, of the metallic, of the miracle of the machine. Dad saw her flicker and sashay in the jerky light of his movie projector which he ran at that young age.

A whirling mass of wheels and light became his first flutter, which would lead to a migratory flight towards a far different world where the farm field would harden into a grimy factory floor, and the soft swishing of corn tassels would become the hissing and pounding of presses.

They grew up fast then. At age ten, Dad ran that Star Theatre. He ran it all. Single employee, ten years old. I know that seems incredible in a day when we still hire babysitters for ten-year olds. But I know Dad did it, because my Dad told me. And my Dad never told me a lie. (I do think he was tempted to cheat a little in cards and checkers—he always beat me—but I never caught him cheating.)

Here are the three amazing facts of a ten-year-old running a movie theatre: first, he sold the tickets. No credit cards around, he was trusted with the cash, almost all coins. Cost of a ticket--10¢. I can see the child's head and shoulders, not much higher than the shelf in the booth on Limestone Street, the main street in town—pretty important. When a quarter was plopped down he would quickly slide back a nickel and a dime, and then tear a ticket off a large circular roll that lay on the shelf to his right. The moviegoers would walk the long hallway leading back between the post office and the printing shop and into the lobby of Gaffney's only theatre, the Star.

Tickets sold, Dad ran (*ran* is his word) back to the munching booth in the lobby and sold some of the basic snacks that we still chomp on in theatres today—candy and popcorn. Big Buster and Jolly Time popcorn, and only three years earlier, Cracker Jacks had placed caramelized corn in a box and "a prize in every package." I remember getting a tiny magnifying glass that I kept, and other small things that I considered junk. That wouldn't stop me from ripping open the package and dumping out the corn to get to the trinket. Always the hope of youth.

Candy booth closed, Dad ran up the side steps, cut across to the projection booth, and threw the switch on the projector which he had set up beforehand.

What happened then, let's imagine. A ten year old up on a boxed-in platform, watching the miracle of movement sparkle through the dust in the light's rays-- and he, at the top of it all, controlling the machine that rolled out the fantasy of the future. (And at this point I will not break into his dream, rolling out the glistening nightmare of the future, Grand Civil Supreme, that vehicle carrying all of our civilization including our bodies, hurtling past the sign *Bridge Out. Full Speed Ahead!* I will let his dream flick on until click, click, click and how fast can you change the reel.) Of course the clean-up followed. He canned the films, went downstairs to pick up the wrappers and bags, swept the floors, turned off the lights, and turned the large iron key in the lock.

With the theatre empty and dark behind him, I can see the small boy walking back to the farm under the stars that were not yet shrouded, whistling and dreaming of a world bigger even than what he saw on the silver screen.

Where is that farm that my Dad walked and worked as a boy? It was gone in 1964 when I visited Gaffney.

Where are your ancestor's farms? Gone under asphalt or the grey shadow of Monsanto, Cargill, and ADM.

Where are the fields of play of your childhood? Close your eyes and see them. Go back and take a look: gone is the creek of my five-year old bare feet. Gone is meadow of flowers and grasses growing over a fallen stone foundation, home of creatures who had reclaimed this area from humanity. Gone are the paths and the sled routes through the woods. Gone the trees-that held our sleep-over tree shack. Gone the vines that I hung and swung from. Gone the entire woods. Gone all the woods of our childhood, gone into the memory of landscapes rolling now only in our minds.

Our play places have been scraped and shaped into glistening glass and steel needles. Why would I have ever expected to find Dad's farm?

Dad told me he did not like the farm.

"Huh? Why Dad?"

"Son, that's hard, hard work."

Dad's words need to slap me--hard, lest I fantasize a pastoral eden that never was. I now have a sadder, more pastel picture of him as a boy on the farm. Maybe Dad left because he was the first boy after three sisters and therefore the little man would have had the hard, hard work of pitching and bailing before his time. Maybe because his mother was a cold, hard woman.

I remember her as Grandma Glower Face, because that is the way she looked to me. My mother said Grandma Kirby didn't like us because we were Catholics, while she was a wooden southern Baptist who glowered at us for playing bridge and drinking Dad's home-made grape wine, fermented in 20 gallon crocks that sent a sweet fragrance. But Grandma Glower was not sweet, and if you try to hang Gram's genes on me, I'll swear her glower gene resides snugly on the X chromosome, and I'll push that misogynist Eve/Pandora thing. And if I do, please don't counter that statement calling me a male-bashing Prometheus prick who loosed terraforming fire into the world. I won't hear it, because Freud was a psychic screwed-up male prick, and he bequeathed me full rationalizing powers. Anyhow, Grandma didn't hug me. And I did not want to approach her. And although some adults said she smiled, she never smiled at me.

Grandma Glower
Gone your hour
The living shape the dead
If you came back a while
And gave me a smile
I'll take back the words that I said

Remember that—when you are grandparents--smile and love your grandchildren or you might just end up being called a nasty name in a book, and be denigrated in a poor poem.

But I suppose Gram loved Dad. She must have. For Dad imbued and exuded a warmth and a charm that I can only remember but never quite emulate. Enough to have wished to have been born on a farm in the South, if that is where his charm grew. (But don't forget the hard, hard work.)

Contrasted to the dream of the farm, maybe the seductively cushy cruise in Civil Supreme is the real dream. Even if only our generation gets to take the ride? The last ride.

You decide.

And did Dad ever see a small plane wing over that tiny town of Gaffney? Kitty Hawk was only a state away. And did his urge to see all the states before he was 21 begin there? The Star Theatre is gone now, vanished with the farm. And with them, less than a short century away, less than my Dad's time, has vanished so much of our past, so much of our culture. But that past flickers in the projector of our mind as a vanished dream. Not so a few generations ago looking forward they could envision Civil Supreme as a dream. They could have projected its swollen size, startling speed, and frightful, frightful inertia.

Well Dad, you wanted away from the farm and you stepped unknowingly into the unman role as a mechanized indicator species: In 1914 the Dodge Brothers, boys similarly seduced by Pandora, opened their shop in Detroit. Hell on wheels roared out, with all the accompanying fire and smoke. And all on fire, my Dad jumped into a brand new Dodge and roared away. It was 1917, and my Dad was only twelve. Now twelve is young to buy your first car, and more so if you are poor on the farm, but if you believed that yarn about him being ten and running a movie theatre and all, then buying a new car at twelve is quite imaginable. Dad told me the price, if I remember, of $950 dollars. Dollar prices stuck in my head because I too, was a poor child. (That's why I'm writing this book right now. Buy a copy for your friends).

An identical model of Dad's Dodge sat on canamauctions.com for a $15,000 opening bid. Dad must have gotten a dandy, for the basic price for the Dodge Touring Car (as they called most of them back then) was $785. Remember, Henry only charged $395 for his model T. So Dad bought a beauty--beet red body, black roof and running boards, with an assertive white radiator thrusting in front.

Imagine! The thrill of it! A new car in the new age of autos.

Dad totaled his new car the first time out. He rolled it over.

"Totaled it? The very first time you drove it, Dad?"
"Yes."

Should he, should I, should we all see symbolism in that wreck? But don't all vehicles wreck? Didn't the wheels carom off Roman chariots? Aren't wrecks the price of progress? Shining progress, glittering gold wonders, from the clanking shop of Pandora?

Dad, you taught me how to drive. You knew cars. You could fix anything. You even showed me five ways to stop the car if the brakes went out. (Those 1940 cars only had a single brake fluid system, so if your dual brake system goes out, follow my Dad's five point stopping system: downshift, pull on the parking brake, swerve in an S pattern, run the tires against the curbs, and always have an open farm to plow into. Sorry about the farm metaphor. I guess we can never flee our past.

No guilt for wrecking your car Dad, I too totaled my first car—but not on my first drive, *for god's sake*. I just struggled with that phrase, *for god's sake,* because I'm trying to be truthful and I'm also a coward who wanted to suppress it. And while I'm truthfully displaying my cowardice, notice that I also put the *g* in *god* in lowercase to offend less. Perhaps I should have just used my Dad's expression: *dadamabeezer*! But you wouldn't have known what that meant, and I don't either, but he sure said it with enthusiasm. As an etymologically oriented adult, I now suspect he used that devilishly sounding term in place of a curse word. Smart Dad. I will now also start using it.

But more on my guilt later, though I'll try hard not to lay any guilt trip on you, cause this reading's got to be fun! Let her rip!

When my grandfather Thomas Worth was born in 1874, there were no gasoline cars chugging on the wagon paths in America. Four years earlier a Frenchman, Lenoir, had burned petroleum in a three-wheeled wagon; and in the following year a German, Marcus, built a one-cylinder engine that pushed a cart 500 feet. Actually, Christian Huygens might have designed the first internal combustion automobile, in which he wanted to blow the piston down with gunpowder. Fortunately, that stayed in design mode only. But it might have been better if it had exploded right then and there, better for the passengers (that includes you and me) on the Grand Civil.

But just the opposite for this next auto! Would that it was still running, and it would have been better for the world. Now comes the incredible revelation I promised you, the revelation that all the world needs to know. You might have known it, but I didn't until I researched Dad and cars. Thanks Dad.

Stunning!

Stunningly beautiful!

The first internal combustion car had actually been built 67 years earlier in 1807. Most people do not know that, but that is not the real secret. The fuel used is the secret. Remember now, I said there were no gasoline internal combustion cars when my Gramp was born. Then what powered it? That's what is stunning.

And aren't you amazed (and maybe a little annoyed at me for dragging this out) because I now sound enthusiastic about a mechanical invention when all along I have been slashing the tires and running over your toes with the monstrous image of Grand Civil Supreme, and waving that *Bridge Out Ahead* sign, threatening to do much worse to our semi-civilized bodies.

Stunningly, the first internal combustion car was made by François Isaac de Rivaz in 1807. So what? So that was earlier than Ford or Benz or Daimler by a long shot, but so what? What's the big deal?

Stunningly, it burnt Hydrogen!

Let me say that again!

Hydrogen!

Powered by Hydrogen.

Pure Power.

World, did you hear that word?

The first internal combustion car was hydrogen powered!

My daughter made me check this in several sources. I did. Re-check it yourself, then proclaim it to the world!

Damn! We were so close! Two hundred years ago we almost drove the road that led across the bridge to paradise. The road we want our children to drive. I'd drink the nectar right out of the exhaust of that first car (watching out for the heat, of course). That's right. As all you passengers with me know, water vapor is the only result of burning hydrogen and oxygen.

Water.

Proust!

A toast to the 70% of you that is water. Drink with me. Let us raise one on high to François! François, *je vous salute!*

François, you are one of my heroes! You have superseded the Wright Brothers who flew with Superman, my childhood hero, and you have flattened Ford and drowned Rockefeller in a pool of petrol.

But I admit my hydrogen bias. François, you were not pure. No more than Benz or Daimler or Ford or the Dodge Boys. You too knew not what you did. No moral credit here. You weren't concerned with a non-existing air pollution problem. You just wanted to get something that worked, and Spindletop had not yet spouted—heck, the Tejanos hadn't even formed a government, and you probably never heard of Texas. Hydrogen was expensive to isolate at the time, but you got it. You filled a single cylinder, closed the valve, then ignited it for a single stroke of the piston. It worked.

But it didn't work well enough, so you turned to steam engines for the rest of your life. And we know what they burned to heat that steam. So Father forgives you too.

Oh, for a better tinker to have tweaked that first Hydrogen Car into the market.

But the important part--the first internal combustion car ran on hydrogen!

Can I say that again? I won't visually bore you, but please say it to yourself.

Pause: while you say *hydrogen car* to yourself.

François, *je reve*! I dream! May we all dream! Truly you were driving in eden. May we all get back to the garden. May we wheel Grand Civil about and cruise towards the Supreme Dream? The H-Car. Hydrogen! Elemental! Pure magic power for a car. The beauty of a dream that might have been.

Reader Alert!

In the light of the François revelation that the Hydrogen Car was the first internal combustion automobile two hundred years ago, excuse me for the ranting diatribe that is about to begin. As you can see, I'm high on Hydrogen. And I'm also hot with anger at those who know, and deliberately conceal, and who continue to pollute and fill their pockets with dollars which have infected our health. So I am going to go off on a few individuals from Exxon whom I do not know personally, but who will have to bear the guilt--for they know what they have done and what they are doing.

If this bores you, you can skip ahead to my Dad and watch him jump trains and build planes. And to you big time polluters, read on. Read what America is finding out about you, and if your name is singled out.

The Supreme Dream is mechanically, technologically, thermodynamically, doable. Hey idiots-- it's been done. François did it. Way back in 1807, a hundred years before the Model T. Two hundred years ago. And where do you think we would be now if Oil City, PA did not have that name?

I didn't call you an *idiot*. I direct my idiot to Exxon/Mobile and the well-oiled boys. But *idiot* is the wrong word. To say it in a nice legal sort of way, premeditated mass murderers might be getting closer. Father don't forgive them. I sure haven't yet--for they know what they do. They have bought up many of the solar and wind and hydrogen patents. And they sit on them. And their bloated bottoms grow fat as our lungs grow sick. And they, more than any others, steer the Grand Civil Supreme, pedal to the metal, straight ahead even while they see the sign: *Bridge Out: Full Speed Ahead!*

So maybe their selfish ride will last their lifetime.

But do they care about their kids?

And I hope their kids are reading now.

Reader, I break into my digression to apologize again--I know I am chronologically crazed, ripping on the oil industry during my Dad's day, because the oil-blooded planet-killers didn't know it then, when they dipped their fingers into Oil City. If you get bored with my diatribe, shame on you. You've just disclosed your cranial vacuity along with your reading level.

Actually, my diatribe also will be oily, containing words as it does from the mouths of Exxon execs, out of the mouths of those who know. Those who still steer our civilization in the Grand Supreme right at the missing bridge. Those with the powerful corporate hands against which all of us will have to pull to change course: Lee R. Raymond, of the huge, soiled, oily fingers, then Chairman and CEO of Exxon Mobile Corporation, said the following to the International Energy Business Forum in Amsterdam, on May 22, 2004. You can google the entire speech at exxonmobile.com/Corporate/Newsroom. I will focus on Raymond's comments on hydrogen. (Eee gads, Ray is my Dad's name! So I will refer to the oily speaker as Lee, even though I am not on a first name basis. Thank god.) Here are Lee's words:

> This effort [at the Global Climate and Energy Program at Stanford] will also investigate the promise and barriers that face fuels such as hydrogen. Here is an energy form that has great

theoretical potential. But, as the recent U.S. National Research Council report concluded, realizing its potential will not occur for several decades and only then if we can develop a durable, practical and affordable hydrogen fuel cell vehicle...

If those words didn't conjure up fantasies or strange feelings towards Lee, please read those words again, realizing that he knows exactly what he says and does. I have reprinted them below with insultingly bold italics over words I would like to fume about. Sorry to insult you reader, but remember, I threw the book at you very early. And I am not without guilt.

This effort [at the Global Climate and Energy program at Stanford] will also investigate the *promise and barriers* that face fuels such as hydrogen. Here is an energy form that has *great theoretical potential*. But, as the recent U.S. National Research Council *report* concluded, realizing its potential *will not occur for several decades* and only then *if we can develop* a durable, practical and affordable *hydrogen fuel cell vehicle*...

Let's do some textual analysis on that paragraph. I did get a PhD that involved analyzing literature, and this is not literature. It is the worst kind of fabricated fiction masquerading under the genre of a speech.

1. *"promise and barriers."* Appears fair enough, to cover both sides of the issue. But we might begin to wonder why the barriers were not overcome or the promise fulfilled after 200 years?

2. *"great theoretical potential."* Lee's right on the great potential (again the question of past actions over 200

years) but *theoretical? Theoretical?* Wasn't that the first, the very first internal combustion automobile ever built and it used hydrogen? Help me here. Is that *theoretical* or practical? Is something that has been built and run, still just a theory? And that was back in 1807. And in the late 1980s a Foundation reconstructed the car, and ran it in front of a museum. Imagine how many hydrogen dream machines would now purr along our roads, if but a fraction of the billions poured into the auto and energy industries had been applied to hydrogen. (Keep reading and you'll see BMW achieve it in 10 months). Sorry Lee. It is not *theoretical.* Since the first internal combustion car rolled, it has never been *theoretical.*

Not doable, Lee, but done.

And who pushes the giant sucking gas pedal into the floor, Lee, with his leg sweating and shaking? And who has cut the brake lines? And who has locked the doors with all the world's passengers within Grand Civil Supreme? And all the while you keep the blueprint of the H-car in your corporate top secret safe, with the key and the power in your pocket.

Exxon, alone, could jump start the entire hydrogen economy. Its obscene record profits for 2006 were the highest ever, surpassing all companies on earth including Walmart. $39.5 billion! They have not yet been matched by 2015. Take a look at that figure. Does anyone suspect they deliberately kept it under 40 to look smaller? You know how "99 cents" falls far short of a dollar. An accountant friend of mine told me the profit was probably closer to $60 billion. That record 2006 profit surpassed the record profit set in 2005 by, you guessed it, Exxon! And how friendly is this rich company to the environment which they are destroying? You remember the Valdez oil spill way back in 1989? Five years later they were ordered to pay $5 billion in punitive damages. Do you know how much they have paid? According to a letter from Harper's marketing department--$0. And the same letter estimated that Exxon has earned $5 billion from investing that unpaid money.

Unbelievably dirty! According to Fritz Perls, the definition of maturity is being able to wipe your own ass. So Exxon, clean up, grow up, and wipe your oiled ass.

Are you reading, Lee's children and grandchildren?

Yet you, Lee, sit on it, and take our money at astronomical gas prices while you pollute our air. If you won't give us a break, at least give one to your grandchildren. Come clean. Confess to the world and set your patents free.

Colin Powell could have stopped the Iraq war. He called this the greatest mistake of his career. You can stop this insanity before you call it the biggest mistake of your life. Why not jump into alternative energy and become a hero! Transform the world so you can live in it. Or die, choking in it.

Father help us. Father help you.

3. *"report."* Where do you think Lee got his report? That report quoted by Lee, then chair of Exxon, was issued by a committee chaired by Michael Ramage, retired executive vice president at ExxonMobil Research and Engineering.

Do you believe it?

Incest.

Although the report does contain some excellent theoretical statements, the source says it all. Exxon quotes Exxon to support Exxon's claims.

Also of some interest is the timing of the report, which followed George Bush's "Hydrogen Fuel Initiative," announced in his January 03 State of the Union. Bush promised 1.2 billion over five years--actually only $720 million since much of it had already been earmarked. That amounts to 124 million per year. Hold that figure in your head. Later, you will need a magnifying glass to see it.

4. "*will not occur for decades*." Lee, meet BMW, your worst enemy. And our best friend. At Expo 2000, BMW introduced their 75H1 that runs on sunlight and water. What a beautiful noise! Michael Ramage, surely you've heard of BMW? Even if you hadn't heard of François Isaac de Rivaz in 1807.

And in 2004 when your buddy Lee was reading your report about hydrogen being decades away, BMW came out with their HR2 that goes over 300km/h on pure hydrogen. That's over 186 m/h! Now Lee, honestly, do you really think it will take "*several decades*" to reach the "*potential*" of a hydrogen car to go over 186 mph? And how long, Lee, do you think it took BMW to overcome all the obstacles you cited: *the barriers, decades, breakthrough technologies, safety, uncertainties, and complexities*. How long? Here's what the Project Manager of H2R, Jürgen Kübler, tells us: "We had just 10 months to develop the H2R prototype." (BMW Press Release).

10 months!

Cripes, Lee, all those barriers and the uncertainties to solve the complexities that you projected would take several decades—took how long? Ten months.

And do you want to know why this was possible? Because, according to the same press release, the hydrogen components "have now reached a high degree of maturity." Yep Mike, we still need a lot of "*breakthrough technologies*" to get a car to run over 186 m/h on pure hydrogen.

Better get going, Lee. Better roll oil into hydrogen, swear off greedy petrocracy, and join the clean air generation.

5. "*if we can develop a...hydrogen fuel cell vehicle...*"

I think BMW just rolled over you on that big "*if*"; but to double-roll you, in 2002, two years before your speech, Honda rolled out the FCX, certified by the EPA as a Zero-emission Vehicle approved for commercial use. L.A. leased five of them and drove them just like you and I drive our cars with the exception of using your gas stations.

Surely a captain of industry would have been aware that a "*hydrogen fuel cell*" vehicle was not an "*if*" but was an actuality, already developed and tested, and leased.

To confirm this fact, Honda released an FCX 2003, 2004, 2005, 2006, and now, check this beauty out: the FCX 2008 http://world.honda.com/FuelCell/

Honda zipped this baby around the Gotland Ring in Sweden in June 07, with an energy efficiency about three times that of your gas/oil cars. And yep, it does have a fuel cell. And yep, it runs on hydrogen. And yep, water vapor is the result.

I'll drink to that, and from that, and you can choose the drink of your choice: water or oil exhaust. So choose: to your wealth or your health.

So, Lee, please stop oil smearing the world. Do you want to be remembered as the Hitler of Industry?

And just so Lee and Mike and all the oil cronies do not bear all the scorn, there must be a huge connection with the auto execs, though I have never seen it chartered. What lubes autos? What fuels autos? What keeps down the fuel economy of the cars? Since our auto industry continues to lag the world in gas mileage and lead the world in declining sales, they must be compensated somehow. That might explain why the heads of the American automotive industry, Wagoner, Mulally and LaSorda of GM, Ford, and Chrysler, had lunch (6/5/07) with Senate Democrats and argued against making their vehicles average 35 mpg by 2020.

Unbelievable. That was 13 years out in the future to band-aid a small part of the pollution. Go ahead, once-upon-a-time-Big-Three, spume more petro poisons into our lungs. Inhale, and as you exhale, curse yourself for placing wealth above health.

Captains of the oil and auto industries, if you do not have enough tire tread marks on your face and oil in your lungs, enter the HR7, the Hydrogen 7 Car!

Touted from 0 to 100 in 9.5 seconds, topping over 140mph! This car rolled out from BMW in 2007. But what is really exciting here is not speed but distance. The same engine can burn pure hydrogen, and then without stopping switch over to gasoline. It only needs the gas because of the lack of hydrogen filling stations. BMW is actually rolling out 100 cars on an assembly line! Of course the car will be expensive and I won't be able to afford one—unless you, gauntlet picking reader, Dear reader, recommend this book to your friends—but Lee, you can buy a Hydrogen 7 and boast about how you avoid all those pollutants that Kirby puts in the air while he drives his old GMC G20--that Kirby is a polluting hypocrite writing a book like this and driving a gas-burning car like that!

Wake up America! Jump out of Civil Supreme and roll to safety. Can't you read the sign? Lee won't fix it, so boycott their gas. Boycott their ass. Yeh, that's a bumper sticker for you:

Boycott their ass
Till they stop passing gas.

Actually, spontaneous boycotts of Exxon have arisen. The most impressive I received was an e-mail from a CEO whom I met and talked with. He stated that he and over fifty other CEOs had sent out letters asking that we boycott Exxon. He personally (well, his secretary) sent out about 4,000 letters. Keep it up!

But Lee probably won't do anything. He retired in 2006, after making over $100,000 per day, and walking away with the second richest compensation package up to his time of about $400 million. May his golden parachute become Dante's gilded gown dragging him down.

A plea, Lee: Now that you are retired, you could write your memoirs, confessing how the oil industry bought and suppressed patents, how they did all in their power to denigrate and stop alternative energy ideas and companies. We would forgive you, former captain of the oil industry, if you became captain of the ship of state, of the car of state, and help us, help your children and grandchildren, help yourself, help your place in history.

And you can bet your last quart of oil that Lee's successor, Exxon CEO Rex Tillerson, won't do much either. (I won't fool with the name of Rex T until he firmly establishes himself in the line of Lee. But Rex, if you want to be mocked and reviled by many Americans, take over the wheel from Lee, and full speed ahead. And Dear reader, I do urge you to read an eloquent appeal from Ralph Nader to Rex T. Ralph was an early hero until he helped take Florida from Gore, and then denied that he had anything to do with it. Anyway, he's right on with his letter to Rex T. You can find it at www.commondreams.org

And us? Are we going to trust Rex, intoxicated with gas fumes, to drive? No. Please e-mail; or better, call; or best, write your government representatives, and ask that they sponsor and promote a bill to put America on a hydrogen economy.

Can America do it? You bet, with a snap of our fingers.

Watch how simple it is: 30 x 6.84 = 205. That's simple. Done. We're on a hydrogen economy.

The figures are simple: in less than a decade, in a cold war economy, we spent $30 billion to place a man on the moon! $30 billion, mainly for our pride and glory, and some military missiles bulging in some pants. (Hey, could I be the first man to drive Grand Civil on mars?)

So, being mathematical idiot savants, you have now figured out the 30. And the 6.84 is 1960 dollars adjusted for inflation in 2006. Thank you Federal Reserve Bank of Minnesota for that figure.

So, ladies and gentlemen (Mike and Lee excluded, Rex in limbo but kneeling down to drink from the black pool) if we just spent what we did going to the moon, *for Diana's sake*, much of America could be drinking and toasting hydrogen!

If we matched our moon shot, we would spend $205 billion in ten years (we just spent that in Iraq in two years).

And the sign would read: *Bridge Out—Road Repair Underway.*

Now remember that $124 million I asked you to keep in your head? That $124 million the Bush administration has graciously promised to spend per year? Sound like a lot? In adjusted dollars, that is 1/1653 of what we spent to go to the moon. So, if you happen to have $1653 in your pocket, (and that's your moon money, your fun money, not your paycheck or mortgage or college or beer and bread money, just loose change) and out of that $1653 you toss a buck into the salvation army Christmas bucket, you've just spent what the current administration is spending on hydrogen compared to the moon shot. Big spender, huh? Sounds like we are all serious about the bridge ahead, huh?

Bush dropped a buck in the bucket for us--it was our money anyway, and probably just as sincere as that church-goer waves the sawbuck he/she drops in the collection basket.

And Obama, the new promise? The new flop. Because he raised hopes higher, even though he has done a little more, he has fallen further. No one expected a Texas oilman to stop drilling. But Obama was smart, educated. And he knows better. Father forgive him.

And how hard is it? Well, let's start with the cars. Your car. You can switch your car to hydrogen easier than you switched your videos from VHS to DVD. When you switched to DVD you had to throw the old machine away and buy a new one. When you convert your current car to hydrogen, you don't have to sell or junk it. It would work just fine, and in fact, it could be converted to burn both gasoline and hydrogen at a push of a button. Just as current cars can be converted to natural gas, so they can be converted to hydrogen. (Of course when you do convert, the easiest time would be when you are buying a new vehicle, just as some of my hero friends are buying hybrids—I can't afford one of those, but buy another book).

So cars aren't the problem, the filling stations are. Detroit had the first hydrogen filling station in 2000. One opened symbolically on earth day in 2007 near O'Hare airport. California has over a dozen of them, and more and more coming. Other nations such as Germany, Norway, Bavaria, Singapore, and Canada are pumping Hydrogen, most of them far ahead of the U.S.

The technology is not so complex: with an electric cord, a pan of water, and two glass jars you can make your own filling station in your backyard, and manufacture your own hydrogen. The hard part would be to compress and store it, and that's where we need some manufacturing companies to make the simple equipment.

Presto! In 2007 Australia's Commonwealth Scientific and Industrial Research Organization (CSIRO) had developed a hydrogen generator, about the size of a two-drawer file cabinet, that would sell for about $500. If they had sold it, you could have put in your garage to fuel your car and possibly power some of your home. But they held secret talks with potential producers.

Guess what? That means you might never be able to buy it. We don't know who the highest bidder was who will sit on the patent? But Exxon is the moneyed guess; yes, the some Exxon who does not believe hydrogen is a near-term possibility, but they will pay big bucks to prevent the impossibility.

Listen to Michael Rampage (what's in a name?) the ex Exxon officer who chaired the committee that wrote the report that our main driver of Civil Supreme, Raymond Lee, referred to. Their news release begins: "A transition to hydrogen as a major fuel in the next 50 years could..."

Could you please explode for me? Fifty frickin years? I am trying to control my profane impulse. Father help me. *Dadamabeezer!* Thanks Pops.

And why will it take fifty years? Blame the chicken: "We are facing a 'chicken and egg' problem that will be difficult to overcome. Who will invest in the manufacture of fuel cell vehicles if there is no widespread hydrogen supply? At the same time, who will invest in facilities to produce hydrogen if there are not enough fuel cell vehicles to create sufficient income for the hydrogen producers?"

Hey Mike, this is not, repeat, NOT a chicken egg thing, here. The chicken egg thing is an evolutionary, almost metaphysical question that is not in your league to mention. So don't use the comparison. Do you have two bucks, Mike? I'll sell you a chick for a buck and you can go get your own damn eggs. The point is, Mike, the chickens and eggs are already here. All you have to do, is buy them. Granted there aren't a lot of chickens (H-Cars) and eggs (H-Producers), but since we already have the chickens and eggs (not your evolutionary conundrum) all we have to do is produce more of them. How hard would that be with $205 billion in incentives to make the hydrogen and open the stations? Inhale! Inhale the air and the possibilities. And turn on the Hydrogen!

So Mike, free your chicken and eat crow--and you know where you can put that egg. But of course, Mike, you might not be able to afford an H-car, because your energy companies are buying the cowards of the Congress with campaign millions, and multi-millions of lobbying pressure (estimated at about 3 to 4 billion a year), and millions of lobbyists—okay, I exaggerated on the millions, the number of lobbyists is only in the thousands--the 2006 figure was about 32,000.

32,000 thousand lobbyists? Wait a minute. With 100 senators and 435 representatives (frozen at that number in 1929, since it had been going up with the stock market), that is 59.8 lobbyists for every one congress person. (I wish there were more "point eights" running around. You choose the .2 part you wish to surgically excise out of the lobbyist).

Imagine, patient reader, that you are a congress person and there are 59 people hounding you, who all have as their only job, getting access to you. All their time and everything they are being paid for is to get at you. And green is sticking out of their pockets and bulges out of their briefcase when they open it. Okay, a little too external on the metaphor, but the green is there, invisible in the promise of checks, big ones, to your war chest. How can you work with 59.8 people hounding you, trying to buy you, and that is their full time job. 60 people all hawking after one person.

Imagine it. You didn't really picture it last time when I asked you to. Picture yourself in your work place. Got it? Now add 60, 60 people all trying to do nothing but get at you. Anyway they can. Breakfast? Phone messages. Cell phone messages. E-mails. Coffee? Faxes. Brunch? Letters. Cards. Knock on the door. Lunch? Articles. Afternoon Coffee? Invites. Dinner? Free. Drinks? Intimate. Phone messages at home. Parties? E-mail at home computer. Weekend getaways? Why not? You work hard, and you need a break (from all those other lobbyists). They have a place that won't cost you anything. And bring the husband, or wife—or don't bring them—or the girlfriend or boyfriend—or don't bring them. We have lots of friendly friends to supply you with. And what time can we pick you up on Friday? Or can you get off a little early on Thursday and we'll bust out of the beltway. Good? Looking forward to it.

Paparazzi politics.

Imagine. 60 people, all trying to serve you. Royally. Regally. (I know it's redundant, but doesn't it sound good?) 60 raw, red-blooded Americans, all helping you serve the country. And helping Rex make sure that his oil companies got 7 billion in subsidies, in their all-time record profit year of 2006 when they badly needed subsidies. Pass the hat for poor oil. Lee, Mike, and Rex need help. It's hard work steering Civil towards a gapping gulf. And it's harder slapping your conscience shut when the sign, the sign of all civilization, is so clear. Father, I can't forgive them. Or if you are tired of that phrase, in the words of the Dixie Chicks, "I'm not ready to make nice."

We don't have Lee's, Mike's, and Rex's billions, but we do have our votes. And if you make sure they are verified on paper ballots, they are ballast against those billions.

You see, ultimately your congress people will want their jobs more than bribes, excuse me, campaign donations.

So wave your H-vote in the face of your Congress person.

Write. Call. E-mail your Congress people. I'm serious. Tell them the time has come for the *Cowards of the Congress* (I like that one because it has the ring of a line from Kenny Rogers—actually a more polite phrase would be more effective—just hum it under your breath) to set our country free, to put their hands on the wheel and steer the *Car of State*. (Use that phrase—they don't know about Civil Supreme, and they'll associate better with the car image than that older British image of the Ship of State.)

Please, please do it. I swear I'll kiss your feet—the top of them—if you do. (If you're cute and clean, maybe the bottom.) Damn it. It's going to take one-half hour of your time. I'm not asking you to put the H-Car in your driveway, but a little letter? A little call? A little e-mail?

Or a frickin huge bridge out ahead?

Contact the cowards. Be brave.

trains

Notice that tiny title: trains. I made the print small, because I didn't want to scare you away after that long section on cars. Don't worry. This will be a short train because I don't know a damn thing about trains. Not much about cars either. We could have called our book *Track Out, Full Speed Ahead* to achieve a more powerful image of the catastrophic crash of our civilization, but there are not as many train loonies as there are auto imbeciles who can identify with their technical cultural biography. And remember, I am a self-confessed auto abuser. Sorry, confessed but not self-committed yet. All I'd like to say about trains is that they move mass more efficiently than trucks, but they are still part of the same polluting problem-- and solution.

I did want to mention that my Dad hooked a lot of rides on trains, that was before the hobo era of the depression (for which please read the best bio ever written, including this one, entitled *All the Strange Hours* by Loren Eiseley. And as a very appropriate aside, Eiseley in another one of his books rightfully called me --the *asphalt animal*).

Just to be a little bit like Dad, I used to go up to the Western Hills train tracks with my older brother, Grant, to hitch some rides on trains. When they started to move we would jump onto them. The thrill! The danger! We road them until they reached the critical speed and then the decision: jump! Jump now! Or the train will be going too fast to jump. Grant, being an amazing athlete, could mount or ditch a train like it was a bicycle. Not so his fatter, more discombobulated little brother—that'd be me. One time I waited too long to jump, the train was going too fast, past the jumping point of no return, but the fear of being carried away into the unknown forced me to jump anyway. I jumped and gravity and inertia dumped me and flipped me like a fat rag doll down a gravel embankment. Nothing broken inside, some serious scraping outside. Was that how you did it, Dad?

I have friends who are train insane. They got it as kids when they stood by the tracks and saw and felt, up through their feet, rattling their brains, the rumbling onrushing power of controlled chaos. You can bet these adults have toy trains, but since I called their trains *toy,* they may no longer call me *friend.*

Richard Trevithick got the first train rolling about 1804. And he knew not what he did.

And when we saw those steam engines puffing through the mountains, didn't we cheer those old Westerns? And who thought about breathing the ash that fell on the passengers? It was glorious! And you have to admit, you too read *The Little Engine That Could.* And you too, held your breath, pulling and chugging with the Little Engine—*I think I can... I think I can...I think I can...*

And to finish this train bit—I told you it would be short—let's all sing with Casey and take our farewell trip to that Promised Land:

Come all you rounders if you want to hear
a story about a brave Engineer
Casey Jones was the Rounders name
On a six-eight wheeler boys he won his fame.
The caller called Casey at a half past four
He kissed his wife at the station door
He mounted to the cabin with his orders in his hand
and he took his farewell trip to that promised land.

dynamite!

And how do you think Casey got through the mountains? Why my Dad blew a hole right through them. (I really wanted the first sentence to read: *this section is dynamite!* But that might imply that the others weren't, and that would be a big banging lie.)

Like the trains, this section too will be brief, corresponding to my noble knowledge. I wish now that I had asked and listened more to Dad, but I do know he blew the hell out of the mountains. Who knows how it happened. But let's picture that teen-aged boy, hopping the trains, bent on seeing all the states. He went with his friend, Wally-- nice to have a friend to watch your back, sleep back to back on a cold cattle car, and maybe even share body heat in the cold. I can picture Dad, hooking a train ride on a new line going up into the Rockies and ending smack into a mountain 60 miles above Denver. And Boom! A blast! They were blowing a hole through the mountains that would become the Moffat Tunnel under James Peak.

Somehow Dad got a job setting and detonating dynamite.

I don't know if he drilled any of the 7 thousand miles of dynamite bores, or how many sticks of the 2.5 million tons of dynamite he set, or how often he pushed the plunger and blew the rock into enough pieces to fill over 6,000 freight cars. I failed to ask him. I did ask Mom, and she didn't know. All she remembered was that he hurt his shoulder badly and was hospitalized for weeks.

I can see him in those chicken coop-like camps at night, and in the day, working in that crowded, claustrophobic tunnel. Though I have never seen the tunnel, I feel deep sadness looking at the pictures from the Colorado State Archives. I am looking on the faces of dead men--all twenty-eight of them died young while constructing that tunnel. No fear though, for Dad. It was easy for a man-child who ran a theatre, rolled a car, and jumped trains, to have blown holes through mountains. What is death? What a mountain hole? What does it mean to you and me? Blood and dynamite through a mountain to let a steel snake rip through America's insides? Or become a vital artery to the west, or a pleasure ride for the rich cruising through the mountains on the California Zephyr?

Now I don't know what it means, or if there is a moral, but there is a paradox, for we all know the paradox of the Nobel Peace Prize coming from a lit stick of dynamite.

But I do know that that paradox hurts me, for I love mountains. You can read *The Other Edge of Beauty* to watch me make love to a mountain. Hey, humans have done it with a tree. And when Dad blew a hole through the shoulder of James Peak, I won't really engage in the pathetic fallacy and ask, did the peak shudder? But I shuddered later. I remember driving through Leadville, Colorado, and seeing an entire mountain top being eaten away. I stopped driving and gaped in disgust. I shuddered. A violent, physical shake whipped through me.

We've all seen quarries and strip mining, but I saw a mountain peak disappearing. Gone. Forever.

And what I saw was nothing compared to other sites. Not content with a single bucket like my childhood hero, Mike Mulligan and his Steam Shovel, (at least he was only digging a foundation), the Big Bucket in Germany is a gigantic wheel of continuous buckets that gobble the earth as it walks forward, dumping the earth behind in a conveyor belt. It doesn't have to stop to swing the load into a truck, it just keeps gouging. It fills a truck in three seconds. These mega excavators, the stripping machines, rip the earth off the top of the coal like you might blow snow from your driveway.

Guess what name they give to the earth's skin that is ripped away, sometimes gouging almost 200 feet deep of the skin--*the overburden.* The overburden! Cripes. It's a burden? What we walked on and ate from for all our human existence is a burden? Terra firma, the ground under our feet, the soil that grows our food, our very mother earth is a burden?

Mine owners, you are wrong. You are the burden. And your goddamn huge machines are the burden. Actually, you named this one slightly more correctly this time--the *Ursa Major,* (I apologize to the constellation and to any members of the Ursidae family who might be prowling about) the gigantic walking drag line in Wyoming with a bucket that holds 240 tons. *The Big Bear* huh? Is that because of its ripping steel claws and insatiable appetite? And did you know that *Wyoming* means *large open prairie*? At least that's what it used to mean before you unburdened it of its prairie.

Be careful of what you unburden.

So you think your bear is big? Yes, right there in Wyoming is something bigger. One of the largest mega calderas is right by your side, and when it blows, goodbye Big Bear and your butt too. Be careful how hard you claw at our earth. I wouldn't feel badly if your clawing was just enough to trigger a response. But then, the operator probably knows little of what he does, and we don't want him dead. But the mine owners? They know. They know. And they will not be forgiven as they rip, claw, tear, and desecrate the earth to increase their net worth. Is it worth it? Ah, what poetic justice if they were there when the earth got angry.

Make no doubt.

We are the terra-deforming animal.

If a mountain cannot stand against us, can the earth? And for how long? Dynamite does it slowly, and current fracking has been causing minor quakes. What would happen if we placed all our nukes, all tens of thousands of them in a ring around the earth and ignited. What would we do to the earth? My geologist son would laugh at me if I were suggesting we could split the earth, but we'd sure blow a hell of a lot of debris and radiation into the air--we have Hanford and Chernobyl on top of Hiroshima and Nagasaki to prove it. And we actually thought about trying it during the cold war. We called it MAD, Mutual Assured Destruction. That's the Nobel Peace Paradox in an uglier form. The MAD thought might have faded, but the potential has grown. Physical and social potential. And if we don't blow up all abruptly, we, the terradeforming players in the game, may do it slowly, a mountain at a time, a little fracking here and a little fracking there.

You remember the joke: How do you eat an elephant? And the answer: One bite at a time. Funny, but real. And you and I could do it—if we had a big freezer. But the next question isn't so funny, and the answer is only too real: how do you eat the earth? One mountain at a time. And how many elephants are left? How many mountains? And how many earths?

And you and I are doing it. And we don't need a big freezer, just a big Civil Supreme, carrying those relatively tiny earth strippers like Ursa Major and the Big Bucket in a small part of its gargantuan trunk, loaded with human products of destruction.

Father, you don't have to forgive our fathers. Trains were glorious to them! Dynamite was a blast! As a teen imitator I snuck across the Ohio River and bought illegal fireworks in Kentucky. Big ones. Cherry Bombs and M80s that could rip a mailbox open (don't ask) and tear a hand off. Just firecrackers, but glorious to us. Glorious to the son of a dynamite Dad. Glorious to the sons of the exploding industrial machine.

In the *Yearbook of the State of Colorado 1939-1940*, we read: "The propensity of man to battle and overcome natural barriers in his path of progress is illustrated in Colorado by the many miles of tunnels…The

Moffat Tunnel was cut under a shoulder of James Peak…It is a public improvement…."

There we have it—the moral and goal of their time: *to overcome nature and improve on it.* Pandora had sold her silver body and proselytized the world.

President Coolidge took all the credit away from my Dad, and the 28 dead fellow workers, when on February 18, 1926, he pressed a button in Washington which detonated the final stick, opening the hole.

And Pandora's progeny enjoyed the scenery as they steamed along on the California Zephyr, the Panoramic, and the Mountaineer right through that hole in the mountain.

planes

Relief. Clever Reader. You recognized another small title telling you that this flight of words will be short; but sorry, it will be coach class.

Pandora, Pandora, isn't it enough that you seduced a pre-pubescent boy on your flickering silver screen? There are laws against that. And aren't you satisfied that you overpowered that boy in a rollover car, thundered through trains, and exploded in dynamite itself—these moves of yours might have signaled danger to this lad as he grew older. But then, why would they have? All the youth of his day lay down with you. And if your beauty ever dulled from the smell of the pipe or the soot from the sky, you covered the grime like a painted whore. For a boy, power can be more seductive than beauty. And you knew that, Pandora, when you took Dad's young hands, and spread his arms and flew him to the skies.

From a train to a plane--just a natural leap. As I said, Dad built his own plane from purchased parts.

Again, Dear reader, rejoice. By now you are probably getting miffed at that intimate use of *dear* to address you. This is the third time I have done it, and I should have informed you earlier of its meaning, but I did not want to break the golden links of my logic. *Dear* is of course, a sacred literary device used by Dickens and my buddy Ben to jump out at the reader, slap him or her into paying attention, while delivering the slap as an endearing caress. However, to you dear reader, please let *DEAR* stand for *Dear Environmentally Aware Reader*. There. But if you still have a very large bubble and you still feel I am poking at your bubble, I will address you as *Der*. That way only those who have read carefully to this spot will know what the hell is going on.

When Dad was a boy, birds owned the sky. What a marvel then, to see that first cross-shaped machine cutting across the sky without flapping, yet still doing graceful loops, and doing what you and I can't do-- staying up in the air when we jump. All the mudballs or apples or baseballs we threw as a child arched and thudded into the ground. Even kites and balloons set free to the wind soon settled to the ground.

Then the amaze of it! The thrill of it! We can feel it in some lines scratched on paper by a twenty-year old pilot who wrote it, then within weeks flew his Spitfire into death.

Oh, I have slipped the surly bonds of earth
And danced the skies on laughter-silvered wings;
Sunward I've climbed, and joined the tumbling mirth
Of sun-split clouds and done a hundred things

Dad had never read that poem when he pulled the fabric taut across a wing frame, set a motor, and spun a propeller. The poet-pilot John McGee wrote and died the year I was born. Perhaps I was born because Dad left the sky. He never talked about his aviation experience, except for a single instance when I, with open mouth awe, learned that he built a plane. I remember five words, three were mine and two his:

"Did it fly?"

"Sure son," came Dad's smile and supremely confident, low-key response. And he wasn't lying or hyping. He never bragged, and everything Dad did or built worked. Since planes were the ultimate marvel of the age, it is surprising then that he didn't fly up, up and away on his magic air machine. He walked away from planes. I can only conjecture why. Maybe for us, his family. I remember resisting the urge to sky-dive, and choking down the surge to hang glide off the cliffs of Oregon like a sea-bird over the ocean. Enviously, I helped to launch others. Groundling, I stayed for my wife to have a husband and for my two small sons to have a father. Did you give up soaring for us, Dad?

But one reason you didn't quit flying was because of the aeronautic poisonous impact on our environment. You flew and knew not. I fly, though I know what I do: when I fly with less than two companions, I calculate that flying uses less gas than when I drive. It would be easy to call the planes the pollution solution; but wait a minute, that's rationalizing again: before planes flew, how many people drove all the way across the country, and how often? And how many drove to Europe? You get my point. Planes are taking off like monarch migrations used to take off before the fumes felled them. How many planes are over your head? More than 87,000 flights criss-cross the US per day! I could give you more emission stats to choke on, but after starting this book with my polluting 3,561 pounds into the air in ten days, you might not want more.

Do we need another sign to startle us instead of *Bridge Out?* How about: *Runway Broken, Enjoy Your Landing?* But hang on up in the air there—I am not against planes. I just confessed I fly. But shortly, you, fellow flyer Der, and I will hopefully meet in a transport that is hydrogen powered, that insults less our minds and assaults less our breath that we share. We'll do it! That's a date! And don't just cover up with breath mints. But do send a picture, Der.

millwright mascot, Pandora's pet

Dad was coming home from work, and we could meet him! Happy memory. Mom would prompt my brother and me, then we would wait outside excitedly, looking up the long sidewalk until over the top of the Cincinnati hill came my tall Dad striding down. I ran hard and hard and up and up and into his arms.

Joy! Just joy! One of my best memories. I love ya, Dad.

Dad was coming home from the factory. I think it was the General Electric plant, I'm not sure, and Mom is not answering her phone right now to confirm the fact. Anyhow, I know he was called a millwright. *Millwright— one whose occupation it is to…set up their machinery.* Thank my silver duct-taped dictionary, the Merriam Webster, the real one, not the generic Webster. Later on for books and thoughts, now to the nuts and bolts.

Forget it. Don't know nothin' bout nuts and bolts. Seriously, which is which? Although my garage has bottles of metal pieces, I don't know how they work--but I have figured out the nails.

Dad did something for GE's machines, part of the great World War II war machine, I'm guessing, for it was about that time. Those words, *war machine*, say all I need to say about the growth of the Grand Civil TankShipPlane Supreme. And about all those bridges and blood.

Thanks Pandora. It's a lot easier to kill a lot more of "the enemy" now; and does it matter if it's easier for "the enemy" to kill me?

With my joy of war sitting on my Dad's shoulders as he carried me down the sidewalk, came my greatest childhood trauma—the fear of nuclear death. I remember my parents talking excitedly about a headlines and a half-page photo of the mushroom cloud. I remember that photo. It is not a superimposed memory. Possibly I recall it because of the emotional intensity in the room. But that photo later led to five years when I was afraid to fall asleep because of the thought that I could become ashes in an instant, without a chance to kiss Mom and Dad goodbye. And a few years later with religion stuffing my brain, I worried that I could evaporate before I told God I was sorry for my sins and asked him not to send me to hell because I had not told the truth in confession. It was great to be a guilt-filled Catholic.

Maybe you did not share that religious fear, Der, but together we did share the bomb.

Later I met the man who took that photo at Alamogordo. I asked him what he thought at the moment of the explosion, and he said first it was *beautiful* and then he said it was *terrible.* I offered him a stolen line from Yeats as a title for his pictorial book when he publishes it: *a terrible beauty is born.*

Okay, so toss the damn bomb in Civil's trunk—won't make much difference when it all falls into the grandgulfendofitall. I'm not against nuclear reactors if the mining and tailing operations are contained, and if the radioactive materials are sanely buried in geostable sites. But the bomb is in the same car that once glimmered as a promise, and then rode onto the road of crushing reality with lethality smoking from its pipes. Breathe Deeply.

whistling to a wood saw

Dad's last job was a worker in wood. Sounds safer. Don't bet on it, you see, all connects. The wood connects to Pandora's products.

Working in wood sounds softer and smoother than clanking machines. Granted the trees yielded their lives for the wood faster than they were being grown, and granted

Dad used nails and screws and varnishes, and granted he had a buzz saw in the basement, still, a worker with wood was a leap out of the factory back towards eden. But here too, caught in the etymology of his trade name, *carpenter*, we can see the foreshadow of Grand Civil. *Carpenter* comes from the Latin word for *wagon*. Originally a carpenter was a wagon maker, and while wagons didn't blast tons of pollutants into the air, their creaking, squeaking wheels, whether in a war chariot or a farmer's wagon clattering on cobblestone sent shivers down spines, sent signals down to us of something large and looming, and more terrible than any Tyrannosaurus Rex.

Dad was building a wood form for a bridge when a fourteen foot high truck (mini-Grand) came along ignoring the sign that said 13 FOOT CLEARANCE. Who reads *Bridge Out* signs, right? The truck knocked Dad and an I-Beam off the bridge, Dad hit the ground first, then the I-Beam smashed his chest, flattened four vertebrae, and broke many ribs. Somehow his heart did not burst. Not so lucky his lungs.

Dad was told he would not live, then that he would never leave a bed, then that he would never walk, then that he would never work. He did them all, in that order. Tough Dad. After a half-year in the hospital, Dad left with 26% of his lungs functioning. Ironically, the iron lung saved him but he had stopped working with Pandora's metal machines and had picked up a hammer and a saw.

For nineteen years with an oxygen tube pumping into his nostrils, Dad wheezed in the saw dust filled basement. Dad returned often into those *iron lungs,* as Pandora smiled at his suffering. Was Pandora getting revenge for his desertion? Could he desert her? Can any of us ever desert her? But he was happier than with his former projectors or cars or trains or planes or dynamite or with metal millwright work. You could hear his happiness as he whistled while he measured and cut and glued and nailed.

I won't talk much about Dad's suffering, cause he wouldn't have liked it. Ask Mom, though, who for nineteen years lay beside him at night, hearing him gasping, wheezing, coughing, gurgling—she told me that any one of those nights, any one of those breaths, could have been his last.

Here's to Mom! Nineteen years of amazing loyalty and love!

I'll tell you how Dad died, because it was warm and beautiful, and right in-your-face, Pandora. After he had just come out of a lung machine for about his seventh time, I asked him:

"Dad, do you want to go through all this if it happens again?"

He looked up at me, gaunt like Don Quixote, and replied:

"Damn that's a hard question, Son." He paused, then said: "No I don't. I really don't."

Dad talked to Mom, and for the first time they discussed his death. He had been staying alive for her until she could accept his death, and when the next episode of blocked lungs came, he passed, free forever from Pandora's sickly kiss of CPR.

What a love story! Forget their yelling arguments. Wheezing for breath for nineteen years for his wife, because he loved her.

Dad was a man.

A hell of a lot more man than I.

I've already told my wife to let me go fast. If my brain is gone and I'm beyond salvage, send me. (I won't let her read this book lest she offer it as proof that my brain is gone, and act on that statement.)

Pain is only for healing. If I'm not going to recover, don't keep me in misery. I'll be happy that I've died semi-naturally before Civil smashes through the sign at the tipping point.

But our kids! Our kids. Think of our kids. Can we help them before Pandora whacks them with an I-Beam girder, or weakens their minds as they cruise in Civil, seemly safe, sucking the fumes? And what of the world around them? What of the beauty forever fled, as they speed through the grayness toward the gulf?

Dad, I am trying to turn my living around, but as you said when you finally quit smoking: "That's the hardest thing I have ever done."

I haven't done it yet.

It is the hardest thing I will do.

I am hooked.

Our whole culture is hooked.

The hooks, billions of tiny invisible ones, catch my cells as surely as the nicotine nestled in yours, Dad.

I am addicted. We are addicted. Breaking free could be the hardest thing we have ever done. Just thinking about it now, and looking days and decades forward, it looms hugely harder than any of my five surgeries (nothing too serious—whack off part of a toe or so). Our addiction is stronger than nicotine, alcohol, food, or sex (those drives can be addictions). My addiction is harder to break than leaving the seminary or breaking engagements, don't worry—having a flaky love record, I did not give engagement rings. Those were substantial wrenching emotional and life-style change, but our current addiction is deeper and stronger and bigger.

How big is Civil? Can we jump out of a hurtling car? If we were born in a brothel, or our dad was a pimp and our mom a whore, we could leave that life. But how can we leave our mechanical technological chemical culture when it covers the earth? After all, the car is Grand Civilization, and it wraps us so totally, tightly as if we were shrink-wrapped in smothering luxury. Grand Civil gobbles and swills what the world consumes, headlights staring at us through our computer screen and flicking its brights as we run to the garage, to our own nano civil replica twenty seconds from our desk.

Let's assume the truth for a moment that the whole damn group of drivers is drunk, and we want off. And let's assume we suck up the courage to jump, roll, take the bruises and pains of outcasts—and then walk, not drive, into the woods? Where are these woods? Are there enough left to support many of us? Where are we? Wherever we are, can we blind our minds' eyes to the sign that we know spells doom to our heirs who are still on Civil?

So if stepping out of our culture is neigh impossible, do we stay? And how do we stay? Do we scream at all the comfortable occupants of Supreme? Do we work like fifth column internal moles to bring the machine to a halt? Do we rationalize our hypocrisy that we remain aboard to convince the others to stop the madness? To change directions? To quit sucking, stop blowing, and start breathing clean energy?

H-energy!

We can change the whole damn course of civilization? If we come together and get off oil and coal, demand that big money be removed from political campaigns.

Don't worry, Der, I have not asked you to sign a contract—yet.

I'm just sucking and blowing a lot of my own words trying to screw my courage to some kind of sticking point.

But that's not our problem, is it, Der?

Because after all we're going to shunt that little problem of changing our culture's energy usage onto our kids, in a later part of the book, and in a later part of our life, aren't we?

But start thinking about a necessary shift anyway, because maybe we could give our kids a little help in catalyzing their cultural sea change. We owe it to them, for

Father, we are knowing more fully day by day, word by word, breath by breath, what we do.

Dad, I forgive you, for you knew not what you did. Dad, I love you. You didn't read books, you just watched Liberace, because you loved dancing. You had no chemical, or biological knowledge. You didn't know the periodic table or a cell or a neuron. You did have a wizard's ability to meld metal and cope wood; and unknowingly, you helped Pandora swell and set up her shops around the world. Your generation helped her. Most of them, like you Dad, fled the farm. They knew not what they did.

Father, forgive most of our fathers, for they knew not what they had done.

And Dad, dying as you did, chest partially crushed by an I-beam girder, lungs filled with emphysema and pleurisy from smoking, would you have left the farm? Seeing the end of it all, if you could have chosen then as you were dying, would you have done the same? I don't know. But I do know that knowing only what you knew then, surely you would have chosen the same. Who wouldn't have taken the keys and the title to a brand new red, white, and black wonder car, mounted the thundering train, soared into boundless blue air on the wings of a plane, blasted holes in mountains, pumped steel and death into the war machine, and plugged lightning into electric saws to equal the force of many biceps?

Who wouldn't have?

I would have. I did. But with what little life I have left, maybe I will stop doing some of those harms. At least I'll think and write about not doing them, and thus masturbate my conscience. And maybe I can talk you, Der, into not doing them, like all good preachers of little practice.

Dad I love you.

Dad, you knew not what you did.

Neither did your fathers.

And Der, your fathers and mothers, in their own ways, in their own life paths, they all rushed to ride on Civil Supreme. It was their dream. They did it.

And our parents took us along for the ride. And we loved it. And they were proud to show us their glistening machines. And we wanted them. And we grew up looking on our driving license and owning a car as one of our major passages into adulthood. How could that be bad? At that point we knew no guilt. We weren't even aware when we lost our innocence in the back of a car. We were cruising in Civil and loving it. The generational seduction of Pandora was so subtle that we did not know we had succumbed. Pandora, the pederast, the seducer, smiled.

And what did she give us in return? Better housing and a wired world. But as Aldo Leopold asks, was the exchange worth losing the passenger pigeons? Do our comforts "add as much to the glory of the spring?"

the great white out

The giant car hums smoothly,
drumming the passengers into oblivion.
headlights swallow the asphalt

Bridge Out.

Twenty, thirty, forty yards or years away,
Stone, steel, death gapes.
We cruise cushy towards the smashing death of
civilization.
Father don't forgive us, if we don't find out.

Hey, Der! It's our time! It's you and me. Now we
get to brag. *Take our hand, we'll drive that promised land.*
"Mama mia! Mama mia! What have we done?"

That cry came from a childhood friend of mine when we returned to the field behind our house and saw it on fire. We had left a can behind filled with burning straw. My friend felt helpless.

Mama mia! Mama mia! What have we done to our world? Can we say with our fore-parents that we also did not know what we had done? Maybe for a time--at least in our youth we could, when we cruised for chicks or chips or guys or soda or the Big Boy, the predecessor to the Big Mac. The car was the symbol of our youth, our speed, our freedom, and our burgeoning manhood as we breezed along no more guilty than the child who was never told of the hungry in India and China. The miles of exhaust meant nothing since there were no carbon counters, still aren't, on our dashboard; but slowly as the roads stretched into years, we might have read about a few wild demonstrations from a tree hugger, and we might have had a conscience tug--I have had those flashes of awakenings in this Great White Out, blurred by books seemingly as numerous as snow-flakes, but after those moments of vision, I have quickly gone to sleep. Sleep that covers the raveled sleeve of my conscience. Thanks Will.

White Outs rarely occur in our clime, though I would like to think I was in one, once in a field in rural Ohio. I looked and saw only white, not blizzard white, but spreading, swallowing, elusively glowing white, almost exhilaratingly so. I could not be lost in taking a shortcut through fields and woods I knew, and besides, roads were less than two miles away in every direction. I gloried in the seducing whiteness until hours of wandering I stumbled out close to my starting point, and I still had hours of walking home.

The true white outs occur in Antarctica when snowflakes seem suspended in the air, each flake a center of light, refracting white light in all directions, diffusing it so all sense of distance is lost. White confusion. White blindness. Lost. Stumbling. The only sense of direction is down. And down is not good enough to get you back to your shelter or across the Pole. My generation is lost in white knowledge, directionless of purpose.

But scientists aren't lost. Scientists from 60 countries, funded at $300 million, have been probing our white poles with their instruments to answer the questions: how fast is the ice melting, and how high will the waters rise. Serious stuff, but I have to pat myself once again for my clever litotes, avoiding the global thing by speaking of the ice.

The Great White Out is occurring now. It is our age. We are in it. We are doing it. We are white blinded, driving drunk, deceived, and going we know not where. And I am as white-blinded as most, trying to wipe the frost from my frozen cornea. But more of that delicious image later.

You may close the book now if you wish, before I begin to pound the guilt drum, beating on our ear drums, beating on our hearts. For you, Der, as I mentioned long ago, will help me write this part, because like it or not, we are writing it now with our lives. So I thank you--and be sure to ask for your percent of the royalties.

I was born with jaded eyes, silvered over with the nitrate of my culture, baptized in a tar-dyed gown, and fitted with blinders to see what they saw. Sucking Santa from one breast and Pandora from the other, my presents came in bright ribbons and glittering papers of promises. I believed.

And life was good.

As a child.

Actually, Der, you were born in the same place as I. We were both born together inside a hospital inside Grand Civil, hurtling so invisibly fast that its relative speed, like the 18 miles-per-second speed of the earth under our feet right now, was unnoticeable. We hurtled into a culture our parents didn't know, and therefore couldn't teach us.

Dad, you left your mess to me.

You wouldn't have done that, Dad, if you had known it was a mess, for you believed in cleaning up after yourself (you never left a razor's hair in the sink that I can remember—I have not asked my mother). Nevertheless, I inherited your mess.

I struggle now to peek over the blinders. I see the collision course ahead, but as if through a cloud. I am not strong enough to avoid the final wreck. Father forgive me my distant past, for young, I knew not what I did.

Father help me, for as I begin to see and know I still sin, I've done it before, and I'm still doing it. I still drive to work. And even drive for pleasure. And I've calculated the tons of that stuff I spew into our air that traps the heat and changes our climate into that global process I am not mentioning.

An Inconvenient Truth! Way to go Al. A big hit when it was written, but quickly forgotten, lost in the white out. The pain of cognitive dissonance cracks my head. I am soiling my birth gown and my shroud.

I have no right to write.

I live in the mess, yet I have not started cleaning it up vigorously like my father would have done if he had known.

Let me, who is with guilt, swallow the first stone.

Help, Der. It's in your own self-interest, too. As a passenger on Grand Civil Supreme you are caught with me. And I don't know if I have the will, or the means, or the guts to get off. If I jump from Civil, as I did a boy off the train, will the huge wheels not crush me? And if I can jump out far enough to miss those gigantic whirling avalanching walls of rubber, will the speed be too great to let me roll away and only scrape skin?

Will you hold my hand and jump with me? And if not, damn it, at least push me off like a first-time parachuter.

And if after the jump I can still stand and limp away and hide from Civil, is that enough? What about our children still riding in that hurtling cultural car? Should I not try to stop this monster machine for them? Even if it means changing the comforts I now feel? And should I yell things my neighbors do not want to hear?

Should I not run in front of Civil with a giant sign screaming: *Bridge Out Ahead*!

And if Civil does not stop for me alone, as I know it will not, should I die crushed into the pieces of my pitiful warning sign?

Should I wave the white flag?

Would my death make a difference? Less of a bump than a squirrel on the road. Rather less than an ant. Or a microbe. Yes, that's how small I feel. How can I, a little one of 7 billion, stop this car?

I can't, but we can.

We can.

Listen to Margaret Mead, and even though my kid said he was sick of hearing this quote, listen to it anyway. It is the way:

> *Never doubt that a group of thoughtful, committed citizens can change the world. Indeed that is all that ever has.*

Wow! A group is the only power that has ever changed the world.

Think about it! One person started the idea (*Every revolution was first a thought in one man's mind*, said Emerson), but then that single person formed a group to spread the idea. Christ chose disciples and that little group is now about 2 billion; Sam Adams exhorted his drinking buddies in the Green Dragon Inn at Boston, and they threw a tea party, and 300 million of us drink the tea of freedom; Gandhi got a group that became a nation marching behind him to the sea; King preached to his congregation and called people of all colors to march to Washington towards his dream of freedom at last.

So, a group is the only thing that has ever changed the world.

If you and I, Der, tell others—we can become a group. Then the impossibly unthinkable is possible. That's idealistic, but let that fond idea sit for the moment, as a bright beacon to return to. I'll need a beacon because I am spreading the knowledge of good and evil with a butter knife, and my hands and arms are greasy. I don't want to grease you if the grease isn't yours. But since this is your story too--if I egotistically tell it from my side, please tell it from yours also. Tell it to your children. Maybe they can start a group, too.

Hold my hand, even if you're guiltless, because this section scares me. Since you're sitting right there in Civil with me, I could use your help. If you're not going to help, at least hold my hand, damn it! (I use a hand sanitizer quite neurotically, and it's got 62% ethyl alcohol that has killed, it claims, 99.9% of all the nasties. Besides, it's got Vitamin E so if you lick your fingers after holding you'll also kill some of those free radicals--wait till the alcohol evaporates).

All jests aside, you've got to help me. We must help each other; or we can hire a titanic band and sing Nearer the Bridge.

That growing awareness and understanding has become perhaps the greatest clashing inconsistency in my brain. My brain seeks balance: I believe that $K \rightarrow A = H$. Knowledge into Action Equals Happiness. Makes sense: do what you know you should, and you'll feel good. Hey, this even works for psychos: if you, psycho, know in that twisted mind that the tree in your front yard is going to fall and kill your kid, you'll be happier if you use the ax. You'll feel better. The tree won't. The neighbors might not. And neither will I.

I strive for honesty which means cognitive / active / linguistic / emotional consistency. Civil caroms in my head like a cue ball in an empty fish aquarium. It crashes and crazes my glass skull and yields: $K \rightarrow ///A = M$. Knowledge not Acted upon equals Misery. But misery does love company, so thanks for being company on this diabolically deceptively comfortable ride.

Let me do something neurotically anal and unusual—give a slight structure to this section:

1-- Lost in the intellectual world of the great white out

2--I will touch on Dad's themes to show how we also are nursed from Pandora. Hopefully that will help us to understand the direction and the end of our cultural imprinting

3-- And as I age through these pages, I'll look for signs of the evil beneath the good—for it is our generation that growingly knows what we do. I will look for Pandora, for my own guilt, and hopefully pull some strength from that knowledge and guilt to join with you to change a few things.

Why not take a hard look at us? Our fathers changed a lot towards what they knew not. Our turnaround--towards what we know!

While my Dad could run a movie projector as a child, I couldn't run a camera until digital arrived; I jumped from the trains before they went anywhere, blew fireworks in place of dynamite, puked on my first piper cub plane ride, and I couldn't fix my cars. Those childish mechanical reflections of my father in me, as unsuccessful as I was, still prove my claim that Pandora is a pederast. She seduced me as a boy, mated with me as a young man, and keeps me tied up in her attic where, blinded in the immobile whiteness of ideas, divorced from action, I am still in her power.

My themes are quite different from my father, for I think and talk—Dad acted. I live in a book—that's part of my personal white out. Books have helped me see the knowledge of Civil slowly seeping into culture, and only lately and slowly has that knowledge seeped into me.

I won't cherry pick the bright red parts of my life. (I have done that from the sun-red cherry tree of my youth, on the basketball courts for a quick bucket, and from many of the trees and courts of life.) But I will selectively pick the parts of my life that are caught in Civil. This book of guilt and glory, (the chapter on glory forthcoming in our joint sequel), will also flow with rivers and climb the mountains, and of course, avalanche the books.

I would certainly like to tell you about my childhood crushes, teen infatuations, first love, later loves, break-ups--but you probably wouldn't be interested anyhow. Good, let me tell you anyway about my first crush and first kiss, especially since it has nothing to do with the Cross and the Car, but trust me--I will find a way to weave it in—rationalizing, you know.

I was five and she four.

Hiding under a bush, playing hide-n-seek. Her name, as I recall, was Carol Fisher, next door neighbor. And Carol, if you ever read this, I hope I haven't misspelled your name, and Carol, I hope your memory is as fond as mine, but I suspect it isn't. I'm guessing you don't even remember, for as I was caught in a wonderful moment of tenderness, a moment of early surgings from time immemorial, of human love, of childhood imitations—I pecked.

I placed my little lips on your soft cheek, and pecked.

You turned your head away like it was nothing, and you ran out from under the bush leaving me jilted. But I still own my tender memories. I hope, Carol, as you grew and blossomed, that you did not stomp too many other hearts into the ground. But if I was wrong, Carol, and you do remember and ran away not out of disgust but from the overwhelming power of the emotional moment of your first kiss, then please tell me so I can run after you and place a big one on your now wrinkled cheeks.

But I told you I would probably rationalize and connect this disconnected fragment—as we left the farm theme (my god, we were sitting under a bush—how much closer to a farm can you get?) for the factories (the gravel road by the bush would soon be asphaltized as our childhood vanished with the farm) and I was already in kindergarten, beginning the Great White Out of our generation. So there. See. All connects. And okay, so I transgressed, digressed, seduced by a kiss. I promise not to stray too often-- unless the primrose path leads beyond the kiss. But, I have said nothing really digressive like changing cultural kissing customs—but that's another book.

And all from a kiss. A kindergarten kiss. A human touch. A touch we will need, to touch again nature, the source of all of our touches, and maybe the motivation to turn that damn big car around.

Notice I didn't say blow the car up. Just turn it. Power it differently. Use it wisely. No Problem...

Big problem. Problem passed to us and which we are passing onto our sons and daughters.

Bigger problem. The passing and not the fixing. We need to drive towards something new and better and more exciting—like breathing in a cool fresh morning's lung full with the dew, almost frost, on our toes. That'll get us dancing.

I used to laugh and say they fought the war over me. I was born in 1941. Don't laugh, Der, because I'm probably older than you. (And sorry if you were fantasizing, but remember who you are, DEAR: Dear Environmentally

Aware Reader.) Now that reader and writer have reached the platonic stage of age, the rest should be easy.

I don't know if I was a pretty baby, but four years later, it was not so pretty when the world woke and screamed.

July 16, 1945, in the pre-dawn grayness a sun-dark fear was born. Atom. Pandora's baby. And ours.

I remember the newspaper photo of the mushrooming birth. I never liked mushrooms—icky as a plant. Dead. And on a dinner plate? Portobello go to hell-o. Mushrooms (and truffles) are for rooting animals with snouts. And nuclear mushroom fireballs are for the un-animal, the human. Shall we call him the *unmal*? No, that would disgrace the animal. How about the *unman*? It's got possibilities. That way, Der human, you and I could point fingers at the *unman*. Scapegoating is a wonderful cultural extension of our individual rationalizing.

Those goddamnsonofabitchin unmen!

As Oppenheimer profoundly stated: the unmen had become death, the destroyer of worlds.

Oppenheimer and Einstein quickly realized what the unmen were doing—destroying worlds!

That defines the problem. That describes the road to the bridge-out. None of us, though, sees that tremendous looming destruction as clearly while we sit in shining, speeding Civil. Through our tech tainted windows we can barely see it in the ashes of two Japanese cities. The atom is instant, but the approaching gulf is just as final.

Oppenheimer tried to stop Grand Civil Supreme. At a ceremony at Los Alamos celebrating their achievement, he warned of a coming curse. What bravery! Listen to his wisdom:

> If atomic bombs are to be added to the arsenals of the warring world, or to the arsenals of nations preparing for war, then the time will come when mankind will curse the name of Los Alamos and

Hiroshima. The peoples of this world must unite, or they will perish…The atomic bomb has spelled [it] out for all men to understand. (Alex website, Office for History of Science and Technology, U of C, Berkeley).

Oppenheimer continued to fight on the Atomic Energy Commission to stop the H-Bomb. When asked shortly before his death about his creation he said: "My own feelings about responsibility and guilt have always had to do with the present, and so far in this life that has been more than enough to occupy me." Was Oppi guilty? If I were in a war and I knew that Hitler had a dedicated research facility seeking the atom bomb, you bet I would be right there with Oppi, racing, embracing Pandora.

Oppi, you are guiltless. Far more, you are a hero in my eyes, for as soon as you knew, you tried to turn. Harder than making the bomb was turning against the creator—yourself; turning against your friends, the culture that created the bomb; turning against your own child from Pandora, bright with ugly beauty. That's a hero!

You knew and tried—that is the point. And that is exactly what we all must do–turn against our cultural inertia that is hurtling full speed past the sign: *Bridge Out*.

I know, and am I trying? A little, mumbling through it now, but not enough not yelling and flailing in the marketplace.

Let's begin now, a ripple, a wave towards a cultural sea change.

We can begin to change our attitude and our actions, and then pass the real job of change onto our children, our children who will help their own children swim and ride in safety and beauty.

If Oppi isn't guilty, who is? Are we all pawns of Pandora? Can no one stop the madness? Can we? Read on, Der, I will not leave you without hope. The hope is in our children, but do we want to pass the buck to them, to place their hands on the giant steering wheel when it is hurtling beyond braking speed? Would you first teach your daughter to drive by sitting her on your lap behind the wheel when the needle plunged below the last mph indicator? And then seeing the looming blackness up ahead, would you say: "Here! Take the wheel! I've got you this far, and this is my parting gift of my world to yours. Enjoy, my daughter. And oh, by the way, read that sign ahead."

As a boy I exulted with the adults celebrating America's Bomb, symbol and reality of America's technological might. A few years later I would lie curled in fetal fear shaking under blankets and ducking under school desks for drills. What I didn't see in that atomic cloud was the smiling image of Pandora's face. It is there now. And you don't need a strong imagination to see it.

Japan surrendered. At that time it seemed Truman made the right call as he let the genie out of the atom. Maybe he could have done it differently: as much as I love mountains, perhaps he could have taken a scoop out of Mt. Fuji, and that alone would have made the point, and perhaps set a precedent for not using atomic power in war.

Then the genie jumped to the European countries, which had obviously controlled their industrial war machines so well in the last two World Wars that they had demonstrated their responsibility and their right to own the atom. And Genie whirled into dictatorial Russia and China; into Pakistan with its mad madrassas; into India, nuclear best buddy to Pakistan; into Israel with its ten for one policy; into North Korea and co-crazy Iran; and secretively into Japan with its samurai swords saluting the nuclear. Do you see that Machiavellian Mona Lisa smile on Pandora?

I don't laugh anymore about starting the war in my birth year, because war is a lot less funny—not that we ever heard laughter from the wounded and dead. But WWII was the gold old war (I've gilded excrement, but back then Pearl Harbor was still a gem defiled by an evil enemy, as told by

American textbooks. The gold old war was before the Korean stalemated slaughter, the Vietnam quagmire of horrors, and the lying, premeditated, and therefore the most evil, Iraq war of oil, elections, empire, connections, and money.

farm only a fantasy

Where have all the farmers gone? Over 98% of Americans are not farmers.

That alone is a startling fact showing the speed of our culture, of our urbanized energy sucking, smoke spewing culture, rolling mechanically forward with increasing velocity, revolving with the unstoppable inertia of the earth's mass.

We have stepped a long way from those living farm fields of food into Safeway, Kroger, and Walmart. Think of it. Food packed in plastic, squared, stacked in pyramids, pieces of flesh in freezers. No heads of animals, not too many eyes staring up at you—fish don't count. The smart eat organic and free range. If you can't afford it, join a co-op. And for god's sake, visit a farm in between your museums—just as historical and far more healthy.

I visited a farm—once.

As a teenager I went to a farm in Indiana. I'd like to say I had agrarian instincts, but a cute city girl, Pat whom I had a crush on, had moved out there to live with her uncle. (Maybe her Mother, smart woman, was moving her away from me). I also went to the farm because I had some fireworks that were banned in Cincinnati. I had tried to set them off in Cincy but got caught by a cop cause I was too fat to get over a fence. (Fat helps to roll off a train, but not to outrun the fat cops). So, a farm was the perfect place. Wrong!

Blam! The farmer came out, red faced and shaking. I could deal with his red anger, but not his shaky hand. He held a colt 44! Big. Black. And he waved it at me in angry circles. The end of the gun barrel looked like a cannon. I'm sure my fear enlarged it, but damn that black hole didn't need bullets. It could kill by itself like a basilisk's dark eye.

I remember reading how Malcolm X recommended big guns to rob stores with, because big guns had an immediate intimidating effect on the cashier. I agree-- farmer, take my cash, my fireworks, my ass, my friends— and you can keep your niece.

Goodbye farmer. I'm sorry I spooked your cows. I never knew your name nor shook your hand nor did I ever want to.

Goodbye farmer's niece, Pat, whom I never saw again, whose hand I held and the much more of you that I wanted to. Why are crushes one-sided? I wasn't fat then, but I did have glasses.

The last farms I saw from Civil's window slapped me in the face. Geometrical, paradoxical absurdity. On route 2 in Indiana near Valparaiso, I drove past contrasting squares of land and blocks of buildings looking about as odd as if you placed a TV set in your driveway, and next to it, a potted plant. They alternated for a while like a checkerboard—a square of food and a square of factory.

Bizarre.

Pandora and *Natura.*

Clashing civilization.

What was this mix? Healthy I'm sure—iron is good for the blood.

As long as I'm an agrarian expert, credentialed from my firecracker farm, here comes the real evil in the garden, the snake in the grass, the snake in the seed.

It's called the terminal gene.

And the snake was put there by us. To insure that farmers don't keep some of their own seed for next year's crop, and thus have to buy new seed each year, Pandora slithered into the giant agribusiness conglomerates Monsanto, ADM, Syngenta,and Cargill (I think she was already in them) and developed the terminal gene.

The terminal gene! Damn! That sounds like the death gene! You've got that right.

That means it will grow once. All the seed from that plant will be sterile. Sterile seeds? Sounds dangerous, and also inedible. Now, a simple little question—what happens if this sterile, say corn gene, jumps the field and hy-breeds with other plants?

Sterile plants.

That means they flower once, and are gone the next year. Go ahead, spread the picture in your mind. Watch the green come once, and then no more green. Goodbye green. Goodbye spring. Goodbye us.

Why would anyone let a death genie out of the bottle? Why would anyone set the grim reaper loose in our fields of life? You know: money.

(((!@*)_)*%$#*()*(_)(%))!!!

I want to go off on these guys like I did Exxon. May I? I knew you would say yes. Before I do, I must confess that I read about the death gene a decade ago, and I have not re-researched it. I don't research anyhow—I rant. But I have promised and I re-promise that my ranting is the truth as I rant it.

Anyhow, here I go off on the creators of—pardon, the Destroyers of Life: You whoreson mule asses! (I can't bless them with the traditional phrase--a horse's ass. A horse's ass might produce another horse's ass, but a mule's ass is sterile.) Dead.

You mule's ass! You stinking dead mule's ass. May the transgenic gene strike your loins! I invoke my Master, the Bard, to call down all curses from on high. I'm sure he would rage against these greedy genociders, and would not mind me borrowing his words and substituting a few of my own. So Shakespeare, call down the wrath of the heavens upon these Destroyers of Life:

Blow, winds, and crack their cheeks. Rage, blow.
You cataracts and hurricanoes, spout

Till you have drenched their mansions, drown'd the
cocks!
You sulph'rous and thought-executing fires,
Vaunt-couriers of oak-cleaving thunderbolts,
Singe their foul heads! And thou, all-shaking
thunder,
Strike flat the thick rotundity o' their hearts
Crack nature's moulds, all germens spill at once,
That make ingrateful man!

Adapted from Shakespeare—King Lear

There! The Bard has condemned you, you unmen of
Monsanto or whosoever you are for all time in his immortal
words. May your terminal sperm yield no offspring. May
you die, slowly, with balls hollow.

It's hard to top that stupidity, but some physicists
tried. Like kids playing with matches, they created a
fireball at the Relativistic Heavy Ion Collider in Upton,
New York that might produce a black hole. Don't worry,
they "are reasonably sure that no such black holes could
escape and consume Earth."

Escape and consume earth? Small problem. I'll let
you to do the cursing this time, Der, and you too may quote
Shakespeare when your invective runs out.

books not nails

Dad hit nails for a living and played cards to live.
Books were for fat lazy boys like his son—me. I did read.
And I can thank my Mom a lot for that. Some
environmental knowledge seeped from books, and I think
in them I knew guilt for the first time.

Books symbolize our Great White Out: the effete
intellectual, (accurate phrase from a crook), Underground
Man, the unman who knows but does nothing.

Dad was right about me being lazy when I read. I read to dream into worlds away and beyond. I only read fiction, and later I would rationalize that fictional reading into a Renaissance Literature degree, and then slowly, painfully, evolve into the book-writing word monger, to which you can now attest.

I read, write, and talk for a living. (There are suckers in this world who will pay for anything.)

I love books.

I turned to books early to fill my head and to fuel my dreams. Religious fanatics like Savonarola burned books along with heretics; dictators like Hitler burned books and those he scapegoated; and CEO Exxon/Mobile execs like Lee and Ramage burn lives, and I'm sure they would like to burn books like this one which castigates their black reign of filthy green oil-smeared dollars. Excuse the almost redundancy in that anti-truth triumvirate of Savonarola, Hitler, and oil execs. Polluting tyrants know that books are dangerous, and given the relative size of the giant combustion chamber of Civil, books will atomize in their fuel jets and combust quite nicely.

For books can set us free.

We can learn from books, and the Great White Out does not have to be the great wash out, if we can only act on the knowledge. Otherwise live like me, with the guilt of knowing and not doing.

But do what? That is partially the answer we seek.

M-I-L-K—milk. The first word I ever read. Not that you care, but it is better than *See Sally. See Sally run.*

I used to read the milk cartons on the breakfast table, and my mother praised me. Mistake. Just as placing me in Civil, she knew not what she did. All mothers place their kids in the giant car speeding to the sixth extinction. And they didn't use seatbelts then. Yet they had no guilt compared to modern moms who wrap their kids in protection as they blacken their young lungs. So at the breakfast table Mom armed me with the written word. And with words I poured out dreams. And now vitriol.

I was a boy dreamer. I am a man dreamer. May I die dreaming. I named my first website *Waking Dreams*. And I still dream--witness this book—a dream to turn the world around. Can we, Der, wake from the dream and begin to shape a rough-hewn form of a new world, and pass it onto our kids? Then they won't have to do all the heavy lifting-- or wheezing, sweating, and dying.

If dreams and words are blessings, I was blessed by being born before Pandora excreted a particularly terrible lump of coal. When I was a kid, Mom swore Santa would put lumps of coal in my stockings if I were bad. Pandora, whose name means *all gifts*, has gift-wrapped lumps of bituminous coal. And you know how that burns.

I was born before she crapped one of her blackest lumps right on your living room floor, a lump which blackened your brain as a child, and still darkens mine. You see, I was born in a pre-TV world with only a Wurlitzer radio on the carpet. We played in the yards, in the woods, and in the street in front of our parents and neighbors who sat on the porches in the summer. Not many houses are built with covered front porches anymore. Guess why?

It was idyllic. It was all childhood. It was fun. And I'm not rose-coloring it with nostalgia. Our parents liked it. They talked! Human communion as they visited and watched their children playing *Tag*, and the now vanished games of *Hide-n-Seek, Spud, Red Rover, Mother May I*, and *Simon Says*. Would you believe that *tag* was recently banned from recess at one of our schools. Too dangerous. But not to worry—the kids play the virtual reality of *Grand Theft*: rape 'em, kill 'em, and dump 'em in the woods. Beats hell out of *Tag*.

Childhood play and adult communication, shattered by the lump of coal crapped on our carpets--the first TV on our street was next door, at the Richardson's, the family who lent me their youngest daughter to practice my pecking technique--which still needs some work. Initially the Richardsons were popular. The whole street poured into their living room to stare at Pandora's marvel of flickering faces, the black and white images that hid the black lump burning beneath.

Then the Richardsons pulled down those white shades on rollers, drew the curtains, and it was a race to see who could save enough to buy the second TV on the block.

At the end of the race the porches were empty.

Human concourse ceased.

Isolated families circled their TVs like electrons.

The nuclear family huddled, and, like the atom, would shortly split.

The clear laughter of childhood, the squeals *You're it*! And *All-ye-all-ye-in-come-free* vanished into the flickering, mesmerized, pale shadows of once ruddy, happy, flushed faces of a childhood forever fled.

If TVs had come out two years earlier, there would have been no hide-'n-seek for me, there would have been no first kiss in the bushes. And there probably wouldn't have been this book. Double damn TV!

While Guttenberg's gift pressed words spanning time and birthing thought, TV shot successive images leaving no time to think. Seeing, without thinking, causes believing.

And Pandora slavered and swayed her hips.

And two years later, almost last on the block since my father was a poor servant in her sweat shops, she entered our home and birthed a lump of coal in our living room, squared and shaped that lump into the form of a TV box. And we gooed and ahhed over her lethal lump like over a new baby.

I swallowed the lump like candy. Buck Rogers, Superman, the Lone Ranger, and a series you probably never heard of—Tom Corbett, Space Cadet! It was a narcotic. I was drugged. Today I still fight the addiction—it is my greatest time-waster.

TV vs. books? No contest. We know which is winning. Americans watch about 3 hours of TV on weekdays, and you don't want to know about weekends. (American Time Use Survey, June 2014). Now do they read? You know the answer to that--if you are over 75 you read about an hour a day. If you are 15 to 19 you read about 4, yes that is four, FOUR minutes a day on week ends. Maybe the Great White Out, named for its literary and environmental awareness, is a misnomer. I apologize. (But not you Der--the fact that your are reading this great book shows that you are among the aristocracy in the Great White Out.)

And yet I think the Great White Out, even with the TV, holds a weak glimmer of hope because we can read-- read that sign ahead. White Out is for words, words that, like the Antarctica blizzard, distort all perception and obliterate our conscience. Even so, sickly, slowly into our generational awareness has crept that terrible knowledge of what we have done, are doing, and the more terrible cultural inertia, stronger than any prison, that is hurtling us towards…

So what were some of the early warning signs, the holy green books that should have awakened us faster? These are the ones that brushed my mind, only too lightly like a feather. That was not the books' fault—it was mine.

1962. A great year and I missed it. I was tucked away in a monastery on my knees and I was unaware when *Spring* slipped *Silently* from the mind of Rachael Carlson. *The Sea Around Us* had washed unknown against the shores of the unmen, but *Silent Spring* struck like a tsunami of DDT. It rushed up the Potomac and lapped against the White House walls. President Kennedy read it, asked his Science Advisory Committee to look into it. Environmental legislation ensued.

Wow! The power of the word. Not so silent. And I have the gall to refer to this verbal realm negatively, as my failing, as The Great White Out—as intellectualizing without acting, as knowing without doing, in other words: conscious crime and knowledgeable sin. I became an English teacher rather than a chemist to indulge myself and lose myself in white out fantasies. Good choice: if a chemist, I probably would not be writing this book but building the D-bomb and blowing up the world instead of trying to get you to save it. Emphasis on *you.*

I've already admitted to being a sniffer—control your images you SOB—I admitted to sniffing gasoline fumes. I also sniffed DDT. Dupont put a nice scent into it. We had those plunge squirters, that looked a little bit like the male anatomy, and I would go around the living room squirting poison into the air, following it with deep breaths.

Maybe those disorienting fumes led to my later love of poetry, for also in the 1960's, Hopkins, Wordsworth, Emerson, and Whitman sang nature into my being. The "juice and joy" of spring surged green in my veins and my heart responded, leaping up at the rainbow. I can still hear Wordsworth's sounding cataract calling me, haunting me "like a passion: the tall rock, the mountain, and the deep and gloomy wood, their colours and their forms, were then to me an appetite; a feeling and a love…"

And I still joy and leap and shiver with Browning's:

> ….wild joys of living
> The leaping from rock to rock
> The cool silver shock
> of a plunge in a pools living water.

"So may it ever be, or let me die," but that crotchety turncoat Wordsworth, who wrote those words, lost his fire in his old age and did not burn out soon enough.

1968. Dr. Paul Erlich blew some of that romanticism out of my brain. His book, *The Population Bomb*, exploded into the terrible but true equation: population = pollution.

I hate to connect my life and yours to pollution. But that is the connection. People pollute. I pollute. You pollute. Let's salute to all who pollute. That's all of us. And more people, pollute more.

The population bomb affected me, my wife, and my unborn children—we held ourselves to two kids though we both wanted more. Two was the magic number then. If a young mother went into a supermarket with three or four young ones, she got dirty looks. I remember a comment from a stranger in the supermarket looking at my two sons in the basket: "Disgusting!"

Twelve years later when we took a look at our two sterling teens, we decided rightly that they would do more good than harm. Clearly my wife's beauty had transformed my ugly--one son is working with the salmon and steelhead on the Pacific Coast, and the other is teaching and researching geology--the ground under our feet. So we doubled our "disgusting deed"—we have four kids. One is a conservation biologist finishing a PhD, the other has worked for the Sierra club. Pretty disgusting, huh?

But if you had more than 2.2 children, or whatever the hell the number is to maintain equilibrium, I will shortly let you borrow my many rationalizations why I too crossed that sensible line and pressed a little harder on the gas pedal of Civil.

The U.S. population rolled over to 300,000,000, probably around October 19, 2006. If you want the stunning larger picture, in the first millennium the world's population increased about 38% to 275 million. Over the last millennium, ending in the year 2000, it jumped to about 7.6 billion. The increase was 2200%! That is about 60 times faster than the growth of the first millennium!

And to make your claustrophobia more intense, most of that growth occurred recently—check my family again, as the measure, of course, of umanity--oops, I mean humanity. When Grandpa Tom was born in 1874, the U.S had about 39 million people and the world had about 1.3 billion. At my Dad's birth the U.S. was 64 million and the world about 1.6 billion (starting to climb), and at my birth in 1941 there were 132 million people in the U.S. to greet me, and 2.3 billion in the world—and I preceded the baby boomers! If you project that rate of growth into the future it goes off the scale—and off the earth. And that's all from Grandpa to me!

My Dad had six kids—the one who was stillborn is obviously writing this book. Father forgive my father, he knew not of the population bomb, but he certainly knew what he was doing in bed!

Actually the P-Bomb book did have the personal impact—it partially blew away our goal for a large family. We held our pact to have only two kids for 12 years until I weakened, and we had two more. I promised you the reasons, so here are the rationalizations: first, cause I'm weak. Second, because my wife came from a family of eleven kids, and she wanted more; she is wonderfully warm and mothering, and children are lucky to be born to her--therefore, she deserves as many children as she can mother. Third, as I mentioned, we took a look at our two older sons and said, "Not bad." Fourth, we arrogantly thought of all the babies born in more negative environments who were adding to the P-bomb, and we thought that our damn lucky condition and genes should also contribute to the P-bomb. I know that seems terrible, but that was my thinking then. I cringe when I think it now, but I'd do it again. Fifth—and this is the real reason: we concluded that our children had a good chance of adding more to the world than they took away from it. So we thought we could have two more. Sixth—aren't you glad there is not a sixth?

There is a sixth. Gottcha! And no, it was not to prove my virility. I will not attempt that impossibility, although I do have some big dreams in writing this book (wait till the end). The sixth is that my wife Margaret is beautiful and I love her and I just could not restrain from giving her what she wanted. (I hope she does not read this book, or she may stop giving me what I want. As a prophylactic, I have advised her that this is a vulgar tirade from a frustrated, ranting old man.)

Since I have added powder to the P-bomb, I would like to continue to exonerate myself: while our parents averaged eight and a half kids (my brother Dave is the half, and Margaret will have to pick which one of her siblings to insult) we have cut that number by more than half. Now if you, younger generation, likewise cut it more than half, the population will be unsustainable. There. How's that for that damn word you kids throw around all the time— *unsustainability.* But I'm speaking to other kids to control the P-bomb, not mine or yours Der, cause we want grandkids! I want to show them the proper way to chop a tree down, and how to lay rubber, and how to speed shift.

But in having two more children, I didn't realize I was having ten more: I failed to factor in the per capita polluting stats of our country—we were in the hyper polluting U.S. with its cosmetically glistening cities sitting on sewers that still spew, especially in times of storms, raw fecal and deadly chemicals into our rivers and lakes and oceans. Per citizen we pollute about fives times more than the world's average. That's how my two children became ten.

Okay my kids, we have laid a heavy burden on you. Not only do you have to care for your own footprint, but also for four others. Oh yeh, and fix the mess that your parents are leaving behind. But if you are as smart as I think you are, you have probably not read this far.

The formula for a successful life is: *Leave the world a little better than when you entered it.* (That was our criteria for having more children.) If you do that Der, you can die peacefully, knowing that you've left me behind breathing better because you have lived. So break the bad news, I mean the challenge, to your kids.

A paradoxical part of the P-bomb was one of the earliest major use of the word *"Green,"* as in *"The Green Revolution."* No, that was not a youthful rebellion (hopefully that is still coming), but the biodevelopment of the IR8 rice which filled the Punjab of India and then the breadbasket of Southeast Asia. So where is the paradox? To feed the crowd, the green food revolution exploded the P-Bomb: more people ate and lived and propagated. As the rice yield declined, more water and more fertilizer was poured on the crops. The IR8 would no longer feed the world, but not to fear. We are going to do it again in an endless cycle of idiocy. We have mapped the rice genome, and some bio-nuts are working on a C4 rice with a different carbon photosynthesis that will probably need more water and more fertilizer as it declines—the second, pale green revolution with a new cycle of more food and more people.

Don't get me wrong. I like people. I sometimes think I am one myself. But isn't it easier to politely guide population than to feed it? There is the problem of the unhealthy and the poor propagating faster than some others. (Like me and you.) But I'm not going to carry the giant sterile inoculating needle around. I do like to play god, but only when the game is easier. Like fixing the earth. But I think education and incentives and anti-poverty programs would go a long, long way. Further than IR8 and C4.

While Erlich was throwing population bombs at families like mine with too many children, *The Whole*

Earth Catalog came out. As I held the big book excitedly with appreciating eyes, it seemed to validate the purpose and movement of the entire sixties. After all, it was a big book, and I had forgotten Callimachus: "a big book is a big evil." (Damn, I'd better shorten this evil). Latent in the earth theme of *The Whole Earth Catalog* lay the soft cruel undercutting hand of Pandora: Stewart Brand, the editor, rashly proclaimed: "We are as gods and might as well get good at it."

That was the same arrogance that Christian theology had inherited from the Jews: "Let them have dominion...over all the earth." Christians populated the industrial powerful western world, so they did their job.

But the next year at Woodstock, Joni Mitchell once more made us creatures, golden ones at that, as her lyrics rang: "We are stardust we are golden and we've got to get ourselves back to the garden."

That song so fired up the literary PhD English candidates at Northwestern that they sang it, off key, walking along Lake Michigan. They liked the metaphors. And they loved to be called *stardust and golden* with pure beginnings, and they had the urge to return somewhere, if not back to the garden, at least back to Camelot and the pre-Viet Nam years.

I never got back to the garden. I'm still not there, but I am trying a little. Although it doesn't salve my conscience one bit now, I did plant my first garden in the clay soil of Texas three years later; but Abilene, Texas, with a huge Air Force Base, a Texas Instrument plant rolling out their famous calculators, and drying oilfields, was no garden city. I tried a few more gardens, relatively successful, and mainly for food instead of the environment which said: Eat locally. And last year I tried to undo all my past carbon by planting a sequoia tree, which in four hundred years would atone for my sins, but it died. Sad.

The mud of Woodstock was blasted dry that same summer by a rocket landing on the Moon. My wife and I were in the Vienna Opera House when, for the first time in its history, their opera was interrupted and the announcement came: "The Americans have landed on the moon." I stood and cheered--as a god--and I was getting used to it. Rocket plume pollution be damned. The moon, an entire new globe to exploit.

Earth Day! 1970. A moment of beauty, but just a moment.

I spent a half hour in a park and watched joyfully as a group tossed an earth ball around. I knew little of Gaylord Nelson and Denis Hayes. I was only marginally aware that the huge, extensive demonstrations probably led Nixon to establish the EPA, The Clean Air Act, and The Clean Water Act! What on earth was I doing, so un-earth conscious? Can I defend my blindness by my marriage, my first born, and my first college teaching job? Important moments in my life, but my life rested on the earth on which I stood and watched the earth balls arch to the sky, all too unaware of the earth under them.

Then a week later in Spain I stepped back closer to the garden. An hour before midnight I entered a Spanish Village with no lights—but it was alive with people talking! Memories of my parents and neighbors on porches came back with a huge nostalgia for that way of life forever fled before the flickering, isolating, TVs. A second memory of a starlit Appalachian village with a banjo strumming filled my mind. Almost the garden at evening.

Wake up! It's night time. On the street where I live now, a neighbor burns hundreds, no exaggeration, hundreds of lights in his front and back yards. Is he afraid of the dark? Proud of his yard? I think I'll ask him. Regardless of the reason, the power draw from our coal powered utility plants is enormous. But he is old and of my father's generation, so Father forgive…But is it my job to educate him? Maybe get him to put some of his lights on a timer, so they phase out? Would I be meddling in his business or doing my duty to others? Does this book fulfill mine? Or will sending G20 to its grave do it? Or when I sell this house and build/buy one that is far more energy efficient; will that do it? How or when can I get totally off this polluting grid, a grid far too much like a paper mache coffin cover that is ever thickening?

Can I jump from the speeding Grand Civil Supreme? And if I escape, wild into some disappearing nature, what of you? Of the world?

The beauty of Earth Day was brief. The oil companies allowed OPEC to form and thus set off "the energy crisis" of 1973 which benefited them greatly then-- and now. They kicked the new-born environmental baby right in the toothless gums, knocking most of the life out of the nascent environmental movement. For a brief moment of springtime, alternative energy companies sprung up like flowers covering the countryside. But flowers, and babies, were easily crushed.

Actually the real crisis was not a shortage of oil, but a far greater crisis of life on earth. For people like me who had slept through *Silent Spring,* it was also the beginning of our awareness of our vulnerability, and that of our planet. Even oil companies began to look on energy not as clean or polluting, but as disappearing and non-renewable.

With an artificially created energy crisis that was big, large numbers of people noticed *Small is Beautiful.* E F. Schumacher tried to tell us that resources should be treated like capital—they are limited. Most small people like me saw that beautiful truth of small—if you have ever shopped in a major city on the day after Thanksgiving, you know that big is bad. But the big, bad people like an Oxford economist, Wilfred Beckerman, of the small balls and smaller cortex, wrote a counter book: *Small is Stupid.* This is what you would expect: a proponent of big business, big progress, big technology, Big Civil: to call *small* stupid. If small were stupid, would that make big smart? Hey Beckerman of the nanocortex and micro cohones, how smart is the brontosaurus?

Hey Kirby, how smart are you? Why did you disappear into the great white out, becoming academically out of it? Momentarily, you might stick out your head to yell at Regan when he appointed James Watts as the Secretary of the Interior who was in charge of removing our environment. Why would a president so loved, so hate the land? Probably because he knew so little, once saying that trees caused more pollution than cars. Yes, he really said it. Even though there is a partial truth in the fact that conifers emit terpenes, would you rather inhale that fresh northern scent of pine for the exhaust from a car's tailpipe? He said it--trees cause more pollution than cars. So the conclusion, cut down the trees and replace the forest with cars.

There's a lesson here about electing presidents with bean-sized brains. We didn't learn that lesson though, for as my generation grew older, they would elect George W Bush who liked coal and had no concept of time, or spatial awareness of how much coal we had burned in the last century: "We're spending money on clean coal technology. Do you realize we've got 250 million years of coal?" This uneducated, small-minded president bushwhacked his ranch and tried to bushwhack the country by dismantling the EPA, and removing the earth protection acts of his predecessor, Nixon. Doesn't the shrub-man like to breathe and drink? Doesn't he have any concept of how his life is rooted to the earth? His name should tell him that. Bush, Bush, don't whack off the earth or any of your small parts.

But I too of the small parts lost the gargantuan insight of *small,* and I returned to my Big White Out—big books and big cars--I continued to drive my 454cc cars wherever, whenever I pleased. I taught happily in college, lost in the lilting lines of literature, and I missed the chance to awaken young minds.

How can a sleeper awaken a culture?

About the only thing environmental I did was to write a demonstration to teach rhetorical cadences against Exxon after they stalled on the Valdez cleanup, which as I have mentioned, they still have not paid the court-ordered cleanup. Dirty, dirty, dirty.

Far too long I have slept. For thirty years I slept comfortably in my academic world, but the 2000 Florida steal of our votes brought me roaring into politics: I worked on the Kerry campaign, and the 2004 multiple state electronic steal had me raging out when I read a PhD from MIT, Steven Freeman, who statistically analyzed the exit polls, which were never formally released to the public in their original form.

I repeat: the presidential exit polls were never released to the public.

In previous elections they had always been released as they came in and were constantly updated until elections were called by the networks with only a small percent of the exit polls reporting. Do you remember that time up till 2004? Exit polls were that reliable, that extremely accurate, often with one-tenth of one-percent accuracy--but, that reliability existed only <u>when there were paper ballots to confirm the exit polls.</u>

So sure was our country about the validity of exit polls, that the United States had paid for the exit polls in the Ukraine. When their balloting did not match the exit polls, Senator Lugar demanded that the exit poll results be honored and that the crooked election be rightfully given to Yushenko (you might remember him as the man who had been poisoned and had his face scarred).

Would that Senator Lugar would have spoken likewise strongly when our own balloting was far out of synch with the exit polls.

That was when, in America, our presidential election was electronically stolen.

Yes, it happened in America, and it happened in 2004.

I suggest you check this out for yourself. Go to: http://www.cielen.com/download/unexplainedexitpoll.pdf

Or simply google Steve Freeman, *Why the Exit Poll Discrepancy?*

I got incensed, and as I mentioned, Wrote *America: the Takeback* which set a pattern for young, bright, idealistic youth to hang onto their values and spread them as they rose in power. Later I re-issued this book with a new title, and only slightly less poorly written, of *Tis for Thee.*

During this time, my son shocked me with a challenge that led to that book. I began to read environmentally a little more, coming lately to Muir and Leopold, and cringing as I watched the dying green fire in the eyes of a wolf. Leopold's shot, which killed the wolf, struck his own heart and was the second shot heard round the world. Leopold quit hunting and began forming a land ethic. Highly co-incidental, and maybe a harbinger of hope, even as I write these words, one of my sons is in Aldo Leopold's Shack in Wisconsin. Sorry I was so slow to alight onto Leopold. I did read glowwarm Gore, and following in his heated footprints, the Kerry couple's *A Moment on Earth.* Also a good book. (Don't expect a second documentary that also get's an Academy Award.) Sometimes I think academic politicians should write more books and run for fewer offices. They are too wordy to hit back hard when they are verbally attacked, or to condense their lofty thoughts into understandable slogans and war cries.

Heck, there are a lot of semi-polite four letter words they can use that even illiterate opponents can understand. I suggest the following: "Didn't your mother tell you not to tell *lies*. One who says that which is not, is called a *liar*. Why do you *puke* before the public? Do you know how to spell, or at least say, *fact*? That's a lot of *bull*."

Ishmael. Read it, said one of my kids. Having read, I too say *read it*. The startling ending makes it clear that we take care of endangered species not only to preserve them, but to save our own ass. The ending is stated far more cogently and paradoxically. Read it.

There are so many great books, read and not read. Aldo Leopold's book is on my night stand. Listen to a little of him:

--Acts of creation are ordinarily reserved for gods and poets, but humbler folk may circumvent this restriction if they know how. To plant a pine, for example, one need be neither god nor poet; one need only own a good shovel. By virtue of this curious loophole in the rules, any clodhopper may say: Let there be a tree—and there will be one.

--Conservation is a state of harmony between men and land...Much of the damage inflicted on land is quite invisible to laymen. An ecologist must either harden his shell and make believe that the consequences of science are none of his business, or he must be the doctor who sees the marks of death in a community that believes itself well and does not want to be told otherwise.

--New Mexico's grizzlies succumbed visibly to trap, gun, and poisoned bait, but New Mexico's fertile valleys slipped down the Rio Grande in the night. Neither will return.

Enough of this bookish Great White Out—we're in a book talking about books. Step outside and inhale the morning and don't worry about the terpenes. Get down, touch, and kiss the ground. Hug a tree. Especially hug a tree lover. And activate! Please turn this Civil Supreme hunk of rolling death around before it passes the sign with unstoppable inertia. The Bridge is Out! Slow. Stop! Turn around.

mufflers and hormones

I told you a bit about Dad's cars, but I don't know anything about his hormones. Sorry. And you're probably missing a lot, because Dad had a great physique, a warm southern smile, and was gentle and strong. And since I'm still trying to figure out my own sex life, and you really don't want to know about that, so on to cars, and yes, that word *hormones* in this title was just good old plain misleading American advertising which I hate and love.

But not entirely. Sex and cars! Come on, we all know the connection. It's the place away from home where… In high school the teacher we called The Skunk made us read *The Hidden Persuader*—as if we needed to see the hidden implication of a slinky silk woman draped on the hood of a car. We got it: get the car and you got the girl. We didn't need the *Hidden Persuader* to teach us that—we just watched our friend Bill, less bright, less athletic, and gawkier than any in our gang, buy a 49 yellow Plymouth convertible and fill it with girls. I lie not. He went by and waved, no room for us. He knew better than to stop. And I can't make this up—two years later I sent my best friend, not gawky Bill, a holy letter from a seminary. He replied: "I have a yellow Chevy convertible with my blond girlfriend Jane sitting right next to me. That's my idea of religion."

What's with yellow? I thought red was the color of fast cars and sex. But it wasn't the color, it was the car, stupid. The car. The symbol of power and money and speed and promise. It was the car, miniature symbol growing into the muscle cars of the fifties to be pounded, forged, bolted, welded, automated and supersized into that massive machine hurtling towards the bridge, oblivious of the sign.

Pandora has penetrated our inner being. Her shapely minions not only drape symbolically over the hood of our cars, they are in the car. Sex is in the car. Sex is the car. It comes with the keys. When Pandora's sleek sexy metallic beast couples with our powerful generative drive, can they ever be severed?

Not a single one in my gang, and there were three bright ones, knew anything about pollution. We just knew which glass-packed mufflers rumbled the loudest, and where that cut-off switch was when passing the cops (they turned into fuzz and pigs in the next decade). The cops didn't know anything about pollution either.

So happy me, in my semi-wild teens in 1957--I laid rubber, speed-shifted, wound out every car I owned to its top speed, and picked up a total of three girls in my life. I carried no guilt in my heart, (well maybe some guilt about the girls, because I was a Catholic kid, and even thinking of a breast was a mortal sin. It was impossible for me to even mentally picture the nipple before eternal hellfire burned in my mind. And the confession line was one longer in the morning).

Years later *Grease* would capture these fifties, and more years later my son would stand on a stage on a hood of a car and throat and thrust the all American Dream. Listen to some of those lyrics merging the car and sex, the power of Grand Civil Supreme containing the promise of Pandora:

Go, Greased Lightnin', you're burnin' up the quarter mile…

With a four-speed on the floor, they'll be waitin' at the door…

You know that ain't shit when we'll be gettin' lots of tit in greased lightnin'…

You are supreme, the chicks'll cream for greased lightnin'...

With new pistons, plugs, and shocks, I can get off my rocks...

You know that I ain't braggin', she's a real pussy wagon - Greased Lightnin'.

I didn't know those lyrics until I heard a slightly sanitized version sung by my son. Ironically beautiful, that son is a strong proponent of public transportation when possible.

So when I pound on hoods with sledges, and break my toes on tires just because I'm a raging lunatic, I don't want you to think I have a car psychosis. I love cars! Anti-American not to. Hell, I even love the smell of the oil and gas. I confess! I was a gas sniffer from little on. I guess they call it huffing now, but it was a cheap narcotic then. I would go into my Dad's garage, (ah, memories of jumping off piles of leaves from that garage roof) unscrew the gas cap on the car, and breathe deeply--now you know why these words twist and bounce crazily across the page. And I am a coward to research the disease of gas on the brain.

When I was 16, I bought my first car, a 52 Kaiser Frazer. You've probably never seen one, for it was a weird car, and I probably shouldn't have mentioned the name because you might make an unwanted association with me. But hey, I am struggling for honesty here; and honesty, like the Kaiser Frazer, is rare and to be respected. I can still picture it! I know you too can picture your first love, but not this oddity, so I'll be brief--bullnoses with three coats of black, dark, midnight, paint! So deep you could comb your hair or check your lipstick in the black mirror of the hood. I paid $40 for it—okay, I was a sluggard compared to my Dad who bought his first new car at age 12 for $950. But I did put another $350 into the engine and paint! And boy was it a beauty! It wasn't a pussy wagon, but it sufficed.

I drove my Kaiser two months longer than Dad drove his first car, before I too, totaled it. I had gotten it up to 90 mph and climbing, on a six lane street after midnight. Straight street. No traffic. Safe I thought. But do the young ever really think? I forgot to tell you it was on a 35mph city street. Some driver, not expecting black death hurtling through midnight at high speed, slid through a stop sign on my left. I jerked the wheel just missing the car then, and the current joy of writing this book. Parked car ahead. Jerked wheel hard left. Front bumper just missing death again. Entire side ripped off. Caromed forward. Dazed. Wrong side of street. Braked before oncoming car.

I don't blame the stop sign runner, for there is a moral here. We are all hurtling in Grand Civil, and we think we are safe.

One-fourth of the car's skin was gone. Fortunately we still had ours. My friend (of soon to be yellow convertible fame) and his date in the back were fine. My date had a bump on her head, and when she put her white shoes back on they turned red. Sorry, I didn't deliberately fill them with glass, and sorry Diana—you can't sue across all these years. So just tweak a toe for me as a memory.

Damn, cars are dangerous. That bloody toe shocked me into temporary adulthood, a state I have not since returned to. I never asked my Dad if his roll-over grew him up faster than the corn on his farm. After all, running a movie theatre at ten, he obviously needed some maturing.

Did I learn? Do we ever learn fully from our mistakes? Guess whether I tested the top speed of my next two cars? Hey, I was sixteen. If Dad could roll and total, I too could total. Just didn't roll. Hey, I was older and wiser. Did I learn then of the Mythic Civil Supreme, and that I was driving one of his and Pandora's little autos? Not for a long long time.

I'll only mention one other car incident. My anger at Exxon first flared in 1973, when I was watching a congressional hearing on the Energy Crisis, created by OPEC. I watched a gentleman named Murphy testify before Congress that he had just driven a car up from Florida that got 84mpg! And then a congressional page presented the senator with a note. I do not lie. Murphy read the note silently, stood up and announced to the Congress on National TV that he had to go and take a call from the chairman of Exxon.

Rage!

Theatre of the Absurd!

Comedy Hour!

Huh? How did it happen? I can only imagine the Exxon Chairman hearing *84mpg,* and doing the math in his head, and seeing his sales fall by 80%, and lifting his phone to his well-oiled congressman, and ordering with an imperial voice something to the effect: "Send a page in there now, and pull that Murphy guy! He's got to be stopped. I want to talk to him, now. And I don't care if it is on TV! Get him out of there now, and on the phone to me."

I never saw Murphy return to testify, I found nothing in the papers, but rest assured he became a rich man and probably drove Cadillacs. And in the way of Washington, campaign coffers filled and overflowed with fresh oil dollars.

On my desk is a new book with a picture of a 9/11 widow, hair blowing wild in the wind. Beautiful. And articulate and honest. If you were lucky, you saw and heard Kristen Breitweiser push our country into the 9/11 Commission. (Notice my picture is missing on the front of this book, and even on the back in miniature. I'm not that pretty, just pretty old). Listen to Kristen connect oil and terror:

> If you approve of our nation doing business with nations that fund terrorists and organizations that want to kill Americans; if you like driving your

monster SUV [as I admit I do] and living in your six-bedroom home: if you don't care about investing in environmentally sound alternative energy resources…and if you are unwilling to make sacrifices in your own life so that we as a nation can cut our dependence on foreign oil, then which one of your loved ones are you willing to lose to the terrorists? It is reprehensible that five years after 9/11, President Bush still has not decreased our dependence on foreign oil. (*Wake-Up Call: The Political Education of a 9/11 Widow*).

A quick look at the growth of cars, and then off this theme, since after all we are entombed in a monstrous speeding car, Civil Supreme. Karl Benz back in Germany sold about twenty-five cars. His countryman, Daimler sold thirty. Ford sent the dust flying in 1913 with the moving assembly line, and by 1916 had over 400,000 models Ts chugging the dirt roads, sending the dust flying, the unburnt gas and oil spewing, the invisible CO_2 billowing (but no glowwarm mentioning here—I'm up to 18 times restraining myself if you are counting). One year later there were some 600,000. By 2004 according to DOT, there were over 243,000,000 registered vehicles. And by 2007, there were more vehicles in Los Angeles than umen. And being friends of unmen, I know one who has 32 autos in his barn—with friends like that, one also needs a pulmonary MD friend—or at least one cute enough and close enough to give you mouth to mouth.

I watched a TV ad that dropped a Volvo from a crane, and gave a Hummer as a prize to attract crowds. They mixed up the cars. To smash a car known for its safety and then to honor a Hummer is either stupider than stone or more satanic than Satan. Drop those damn unmen promoters on their heads.

In a plenary indulgence Father has forgiven us our youth, for we knew not what we did. But not forever. Not for our lifetimes. You and I, Der, someplace along the line, crossed the line. We moved into environmental consciousness and its concomitant annoyances, denials, guilt, despair, disgust, hurt, anger, avoidances, rationalizations, donations, diseases, decisions, and a few other negative feelings. We moved into consciousness not in stages, but in spurts of awareness like jagged nightmares.

flying cars

A wonder in the sky! As a kid in the 1940's airplanes rarely flew over my house. When they did, we stopped all play and head tilted back we marveled at something so big looking so small and stately piercing the white clouds like a slow silver arrow.

First time on a piper cub I puked out the window over downtown Cincinnati. That, if nothing else, should have warned my Dad's generation walking below, that messing with Mother Nature and sleeping with Pandora was unnatural. Maybe they didn't know about the plane's polluting exhaust, but the upchucked chunks should have signaled something.

As a teenager I'd drive up to Dayton, Ohio and lay on the hill overlooking the air force base. I gloried as the ground vibrated under me as steel death thundered through the sky. I watched those B-52s, those armed monsters always in the skies, ready to rush towards Russia so Pandora could scream in nuclear orgasmic ecstasy: "Bombs away!"

If that had happened, more people, those alive, would have understood the still unread sign: *Bridge Out.*

Close by the airbase was Wright Patterson Museum, home to Pandora's winged child birthed at Kitty Hawk. I looked at that first-born plane. The propeller was turned by the bicycle chain right out of Orville and Wilbur's bike shop. The phrase leaped into my mind: *On a bike a plane was born*. Brilliant! I was caught in that technological marvel, and proud of my insight into the connectivity of mechanical inventions. I was a cheerleader hoisting high Pandora's girls with the long legs and short skirts. I was an intellectual leader, blessing and praising the progress of industry and mocking those Luddites, those sledge smashing, machine hating troglodytes.

"And what rough beast slouches towards Bethlehem to be born?"

Yes, we are learning that out of our mechanical sexual exuberance, comes the nuclear baby with the STDs. Don't get me wrong. I love babies and sex, but self-control and population control is an issue. I bought a bike. I don't ride it enough, but then we are only the becoming-aware-generation. We are the coming of age generation. We are learning that metallic kisses, and cuddles in crucibles, can birth monstrosities. And we had better come of age. Damn quickly. So how do I grow up? Should I not rip my hands free from this cross of civilization? Just because I am caught, crucified inside culture, should I not tear myself outside it, and show the way?

An earth loving, life loving, long loving friend of mine wrote: "If the life-systems of our fragile jewel of a planet go, we all go. We can no longer afford a myopic arrogant humanism that pursues its own comforts at the expense of the larger life community." (Finn, *If a Child, Why Not a Cosmos?*)

rivers running where

Let me splash in my river. Hey, my Dad had his planes and trains and magic making machines. And no, I won't float a boat image at you with some looming question like: do you hear anything ahead that sounds like a waterfall?

Where have all the waters gone? The clear creeks of our youth? The brooks and streams and rivers that I swam in? Where is that small *crick,* (that's what my Dad called it) that was only a forty-five second run out my back door. Where are the crawl daddies I used to catch?

I'll tell you where. They aren't. That crick is buried in a three-foot tube of concrete under a subdivision. Crawl daddies don't live well down there, and I can't even wet my toes. And when I press my ear to the ground where once my crick ran free, I can't even hear the imprisoned waters gurgle. The songs they sang to the free air and to me are dead.

So where are the creeks of yesterday? Where are the rivers that now run dry? Where is the mouth of the Colorado that once rushed to the sea? And where is the mighty Yellow, Huang He, The Mother River of China, sinking into the silt, barely weeping towards the sea?

Emerson didn't have to ask this question, because he could actually return to the "same blue" river of his childhood:

> And I behold once more
> My old familiar haunts; here the blue river,
> The same blue wonder that my infant eye
> Admired…unaltered…   The River

Unaltered! Would that we could say the same. The fact that we can't, states the dark metamorphosis from "blue rivers" to chemical, fecal sewers, which occurred from the time of my grandfather and accelerated into our time. Don't let too many people tell you the rivers are much better now because they were able to put the Cuyahoga River fire out. If a water bragger tells you that, then ask them to take a drink from the Cuyahoga—64 ounces daily recommended for good health. If they laugh, offer to fetch the half-gallon for them, free of charge, if they will drink it.

To guide you to your local river of health, you can get a gallon free for the dipping (bring a spoon in some cases) from any of these direct tributaries of the Mississippi:

Apple River (Illinois) • Arkansas River • Bad Axe River • Beaucoup Creek • Big Muddy River • Big River (Wisconsin) • Buffalo River (Wisconsin) • Cannon River • Casey Creek • Chippewa River (Wisconsin) • Cimarron River • Crow Wing River • Moines River • Edwards River (Illinois) • Fabius River • Hatchie River • Henderson Creek (Illinois) • Illinois River • Iowa River • Kaskaskia River • Crosse River • Little Marys River (Illinois) • Loosahatchie River • Maquoketa River • Marys River (Illinois) • Meramec River • Minnesota River • Missouri River • Nokasippi River • Obion River • Paint Creek (Iowa) • Platte River (Minnesota) • Plum River • River des Peres • Rock River (Illinois) • Root River (Minnesota) • Rum River • Rush River (Wisconsin) • St. Croix River (Wisconsin-Minnesota) • Sauk River (Minnesota) • Schoolcraft River • Sinsinawa River • Skunk River • St. Francis River • Swan River (Minnesota) • Trempealeau River • Trimbelle River • Upper Iowa River • Wapsipinicon River • Watab River • White River (Arkansas) • Willow River • Wind River (Wisconsin) • Wisconsin River • Wolf River (Tennessee) •Yazoo River • Yellow River (this one's not in China).

That's a lot of rivers which I have lifted from Wikipedia; therefore, I can't swear to the accuracy of the list, nor even to the accuracy of the rivers in my former home state of Wisconsin. But I can swear to the quality of the rivers--for certain, none of them are Emersonian blue.

If your water bragger refuses a drink from all of these rivers, how about a sweet draft from Honey Creek? With such a sweet tasting name you couldn't go wrong, right? Wrong. Once upon a time in farmutopia, Honey Creek must have indeed been sweet to those who lowered their lips and drank deeply from it. Today, right now, Honey Creek is sludging its way through the Milwaukee suburbs, carrying as much fecal bacteria as the sewer (MJS, 1/21/07). Honey, you're full of shit, and I am sorry that we unmen keep crapping in your once pure waters. What was wrong with a good crap in the back yard, just so we buried it? Ugh, you say? That repulses you? So flush it then--and put it in your drinking water, Honey.

I love rivers, but not Mosquito Creek. Let me commit my worst digression yet, for a mosquito is attacking my ear as I write, and it reminds me of a campsite I chose in Canada on the theory that it got its name on a night long ago when the air hung heavy with mosquitoes. They would naturally be long gone by my camping night, right?

Wrong. A lot of biologists don't know, but mosquitoes preceded the prokaryotes and possibly the Big Bang and will survive the red sun. If mosquitoes were on the endangered species list, I'd break principles and the law and still swat them.

Hate distorts perception, and while I cringe to say it, I guess people shoot wolves from my mosquito perspective.

I'll tell you how to catch a mosquito in your home—you know, the one that is buzzing around your ear and which will attack you at night. First assume the position—supinely on the floor—you've got your back covered. Then expose some warm flesh as bait and wait. Sorry women, but exposing a breast won't give you an advantage, for the bloodsuckers are the females of the species. So just use your arm. When the little sucker lands, wait another 6 seconds for it to get a grip, and then cut loose. Wham. Hit yourself as hard as you can and your own pain will add to the satisfaction of its death. Patent applied for.

There are other missing underground streams and rivers and lakes, not just my backyard buried crick, but where are the artesian springs of Las Vegas? The name *Las Vegas* means *The Meadows*-- see many meadows around there? Once it was a watering stop on the trail to LA. Now it is desert insanity, and water is the drug. It is terradeforming, aquasucking unmen at their worst. It is among our fastest growing cities, and it is in the desert? Does the 4-tier water utility rate in Las Vegas begin to highlight the problem? To understand this sickness, simply picture the fat fountains of Bellagio bulging with water madness.

And when you fly over Nebraska and Oklahoma, do you notice all those irrigated circles and squares of green against a tan earth? If it's all dry dust and the clouds don't water it, should we? Should we plant it unnaturally? And where do we get that water?

Right. Suck it from the aquifers. Even though the United States Geological Survey had warned Albuquerque about water levels twenty years earlier, a former mayor argued for Intel's expansion (Intel only wanted an additional 4 million gallons of water a day—those silicone chips get rinsed a lot, 15 to 25 times, taking 2 or 3 thousand gallons of water for each six inch slice). The crass mayor said that Albuquerque should enjoy the water in the aquifer while they had it. He didn't care if the aquifer would be gone!!! And what, good mayor, will your grandchildren drink? Goodbye Albuquerque. Death by dehydration.

Thank you unman mayor. Does it really make a difference whether the bridge is out or the well is dry? Suck speed ahead.

Wait a moment, there is a reprieve for another twenty-five years: the San Juan-Chama project in 2008 went under the Continental Divide and stole some more water from Colorado.

Albuquerque is not alone. Let's jump to a dryer place. How about the Sahara? Huh? As if the world's largest desert is not dry enough, far below its surface industrial pumps suck, and pipes pour water into Tripoli and other unmen concentrations. So what? So Sahara sucks worse than Albuquerque. The aquifer under Albuquerque gets some water from the mountains, but the city uses it three times faster than it filters into the aquifer. That's no problem, Honorable Mayor--if you make $70,000/year you can spend $210,000 indefinitely. Right? But the waters under those stretching Sahara sands are old, geologically old, and are not being replenished. That's right. Not much rain or snowmelt up there on the dunes. So suck your last sip—slurp! So sorry for such a sick series—I suck at sibilance. Again, apologies to my anti-alliterative offspring.

But don't let the language blur the sand-vast image.

Or the desperate thirst of unmanity.

Or the profound concept.

How about fish farms in the desert? And ocean fish at that? That's what they've been doing for twenty years or so in the Negev and Arava deserts in the middle of Israel. At first pumping up water from a thousand feet down and raising fish and then using that water to fertilize fields might seem to make some sense: fish and farms.

The part I don't understand is that many of these fish are carnivorous. I don't know the details, but I think they are fed with sea fish! If that is the case, imagine fishing in the Persian Gulf, and then trucking the catch across the desert to feed the fish. Energy efficient?

Desert-fish technology? Does anyone see an oxymoron there? Professor fish biologist Samuel

Appelbaum said: "It was not simple to convince people that growing fish in the desert makes sense" (NYT 1,2,07).

Duh.

Where do sea bass belong? A first grader can answer that question.

I am a believer in science. I am also a believer in that uncommon, common sense—of which I, a dreamer, have been uncommonly shorted. But with my little amount, I predict those fake fish lakes will become abandoned, evaporating stinkholes.

Fish farms don't work well, even in the ocean.

Life took three and a half billion years, and about 600 million in the oceans, to work its way up to the present larger life forms. So don't fuck with the fish.

Is desert deep sea fish farming any dumber than Dubai dumping thousands of barges of rock and soil into the Persian Gulf to build artificial islands? Are these Mid Easterners really dumb?

No dumber than Americans. Nature slaps our face and we don't learn. Witness our re-building of sub-sea level New Orleans.

Or listen to the sucking sound of L.A. sending its snaking pipes every which way, their tongues flicking out, searching for waters. L.A. sucked Owens Lake dry, creating the worst single source of air particulates in the country, and it is still thirstier than before. Suck L.A. suck.

Oh, if we had only listened to John Wesley Powell.

Inhale and be thankful, Americans, that you are not as dumb as the Mid Easterners. Just ignore the fact that we fish farm in the Arizona desert.

The terraforming devil has become the aquaforming deep sea monster. Earth beware. Unmen no care. Grand Civil, step on the gas.

When will we ever learn to flow with nature's streams, to swing with her seasons, to grow on her given ground, to stuff Pandora back into her leaden box, to use our stunning intelligence to be intelligent?

Maybe, just maybe, the fish belong in the sea?

Over 1,000 miles of Appalachian streams have been buried by coal strip miners who blew the hell off the top of the mountain and then dumped all the "burden" into the valleys and streams below. Nice clean maneuver. The EPA found heavy metals in 95% of the headwaters near the mines (NYT 5/5/07). Drink up.

And we're in America, where apparently pure reprocessed sewer water pours from our faucets. What about the rest of the world? Over a billion people have unsafe water. And guess what is the second highest killer of babies in developing countries? Diarrhea is the correct answer. And from where do you think those dying and dead babies sipped their diarrhea forming bacteria?

So when your water bragger refuses your gracious hospitality offering them a drink of fresh river water, ask them kindly not to tell you any more about how much better our rivers are. Case rested.

What have we done to our waters of life? To the 70% of living water that is within us? What kind of civilization pours poisons from their factories and flushes excrement into their drinking water? (That was a rhetorical question, and we know the answer—the civilization with their white fat crisscrossed neurons sluggishly firing, the civilization that is snugly sitting on their corn-fed terminal gene altered asses in the Grand Civil Supreme, and smoking and streaking towards the Grand Gulf of Doom.)

Back to the streams of my youth—when I swam in the Whitewater River, tributary to the Ohio--I had no idea of the brown solution I was in. Worse, I swam several times in the Ohio River, worrying unnecessarily about the giant catfish, until my chemistry teacher told us of the fecal chloroforms and carcinogens that were in it. In the Ohio, which bears the Indian name for *Beautiful*! The song I sang as a kid:

Beautiful Ohio on a moonlit stream
While above the heavens in their glory gleam

Who were the insanely stuffed suits who legislated that lie, and made it the state song in 1969? Certainly none of them had ever stepped out of Civil, much less stepped into a canoe, and absolutely none of them had floated down the Ohio. Why then, technologically blinded, would we expect them to realize that black sewer water will also reflect moonlight?

Beautiful river once.

Beautiful no more.

I am sad. I wanted to say I am crying, but that would be lying, but my eyes are tearing up.

If beautiful Ohio on a moon lit stream is hogwash and factory flush, what about the Mississippi? Worst mistake!

I swam the Mississippi.

Once. And you can bet I won't do it again. It's like being burnt--one lesson is all it takes and the water temperature makes no difference.

And I knew then what I did, for it was after my chemistry teacher had told me about the ugly Ohio, and I knew that all that nasty beauty was pouring down at me. But being young and immortal, I swam the Mississippi at Memphis, only later learning that Memphis was the fertilizer/pesticide capital of the world, home to the pesticide producer Terminix. I know little about Terminix, but the name scares hell out of me.

Let me give you the unpretty picture of my river swim. I stepped into the water with my white toes and sank over my ankle. Yuk! I pulled my foot out of the sucking slurp and looked at the grey brown slime eating at my skin.

Even now while writing I remember, and I feel again the revulsion. Why did I plunge forward? Because I was with my brother? And because I had that same damn white western macho reasoning I-can-conquer-nature mentality. And I also confess my sin of illogicality: rather than walk into that sucking slop, I ran and dove face-forward like one does into ocean waves, risking injury to my head rather than let my toes touch any more of that liquid ordure.

Someone should have told me that the Indian name for Mississippi meant Big River. You ain't seen big until your head is bobbin in it. I was ready for a mile swim, drawing a 45° angle downstream to an outcropping point on the opposite bank. Well, the river didn't like my math or angles, and swept me into its own curving currents and I never reached the point. I passed it, the river opened in a wide bend, and I now had more than a mile to go.

My younger brother Dave saw the point passing by, and he started stroking strongly upstream towards it.

I yelled: "No! Keep angling downstream!"

He either didn't hear me or more likely ignored me, as my children would wisely do often in the future. I thought of floating with the current, and let him hit this monster current headlong alone; but since I had a lifeguard certificate, I thought I could be convicted and incarcerated for cowardice if I didn't follow his sorry, soggy butt.

Dirty river water splashed in my mouth. I swallowed. I now know why we drink about 120 bottles of bottled water per American, even though some are bottled from faucets that are fed by rivers. At this point, I wasn't thinking of slow chemical cancer, but quick death by drowning.

When my feet found purchase far past the point, I stood up and felt dirtier than ever before or since.

Some smart people make lists of *Things They Want to Do Before They Die*. Smarter people who live longer have another list: *Things to Never Do to Avoid Dying*. Add this one to the list. Martin Strel swam the length of the Mississippi. He was 47 at the time and posted to the wrong list--the proves he will not reach 60.

I'm complaining. Chad Pregracke is doing something about it. For ten years he has led a growing group along the entire Mississippi. He has pulled thousands of tires and barrels as well as tractors, washing machines, and refrigerators out of the river. You can read about him in the green magazine, *Plenty* (1/08) and check his website *livinglandsandwaters.*

Huck Finn was my fictional hero. Chad is our real river hero. If we could all realize that we are polluting just as badly, probably worse, at the chemical and microbial level, than those tossing their washing machines into the river. And of course we pass the major responsibility onto the corporate giants like Cargill and DeWitt.

Long before you were pulling tires out, Chad, I confess that I peed in the headwaters of the Mississippi and drank café at its mouth. Sounds gross to say, but heh, in the woods, when you've got to go... I peed on the banks of Lake Itasca in Minnesota, and I sat in New Orleans drinking café au lait. The waters of the world wash together, and I and the world had better learn that, or we'll all be drinking worse than uric acid. While sitting and supping I watched a ship float by above me.

Above me? Did I say I wouldn't float a boat image at you? Let me take that back. Should I replace Civil Supreme with the Great Bloated Boat? The titanic would look like a thimble.

Help! Boat above! Big big boat! Boats don't float on ceilings. They don't fly. And gulfs and seas are not contained by concrete. Continents do that—for a while. And Pandora has not yet built a continent in her Shop. Though Pangaea did.

Katrina washed some of that nonsense away, allowing water to find its natural lowest level. Hold back the Sea? Not on your technological tin tin. Even the Dutch, temporarily favored by Pandora's dikes, should have learned. The boy with the cork finger will not forever plug their dikes.

Katrina came.

And Katrina will come again.

And we still build below sea level.

And we still heat the air, melt the ice, and raise the sea level. Oh well, we are the rational animals that Aristotle dubbed us.

And we will wish that we had not cut down the trees which shrunk the delta and left New Orleans prey to the ravage of Katrina. And was Katrina intensified by the unmentionable? (I, who have more episodic digressions than Rabelais and Cervantes together, have refrained from dealing with, and lately even mentioning global warning— if you misspell it, it doesn't count.)

Global Warning! Just savor that serendipitous phrase. Beautiful! Better than Bridge Out? (It is not a Freudian slip, which deals with the not so secrets of Victoria and other sex slips, which being slippery and suppressed I have let many slip out. Sex will out! Zip it.)

Nearing the end of my river journey at the mouth of the Mississippi, let's enter the Gulf Stream and flow outward. Think of it! The unmentionable glowwarm melts the ice which sinks cold water which stops the Gulf Stream. So Europe freezes. So the terraforming unman becomes the aquaforming nightmare of the deep. The once great ocean, image of unending immensity, is now small and vulnerable. We are the ocean. We are the earth.

And be careful outer space! As Unman migration followed the rivers, and then the deer paths which became the wagon roads which became the highways which became the interstates which grew the cities away from the rivers which built Spaceports in Florida and California. Already we have junked our earth orbit, and if spaceship earth continues to bear life that long, watch out outer space! How long? I'll tell you that later, but that is our children's part, our Green Hope, and the length rests in the future and comes with our kids. But it will come, I promise you. It must come. We must have hope. After all, it's our kids, and I think you'll want to bet on them with me.

A last farewell to the rivers from John Wesley Powell who was indeed a river god. He was the first man we know to navigate through the Grand Canyon. Listen to him describe the former beauty of the Colorado river that once rushed in its fullness and now dies before it reaches the sea, receiving an artificial transfusion to let some waters flow.

> The wonders of the Grand Canyon cannot be adequately represented in symbols of speech, nor by speech itself... It is the land of music. The river thunders in perpetual roar, swelling in floods of music when the storm gods play upon the rocks and fading away in soft and low murmurs when the infinite blue of heaven is unveiled. With the melody of the great tide rising and falling, swelling and vanishing forever, other melodies are heard in the gorges of the lateral canyons, while the waters plunge in the rapids among the rocks or leap in great cataracts. Thus the Grand Canyon is a land of song. Mountains of music swell in the rivers, hills of music billow in the creeks, and meadows of music murmur in the rills that ripple over the rocks. Altogether it is a symphony of multitudinous melodies. All this is the music of waters. The adamant foundations of the earth have been wrought into a sublime harp, upon which the clouds of the heavens play with mighty tempests or with gentle showers.   John Wesley Powell

One last parting shot at what we have done to our waters. The Sadhus, the holy men of India, said they would no longer wash away their sins in the waters of the Ganges because it was too dirty. Too dirty to wash sins or anything else. Would Christ, today, walk into the Jordan to be baptized?

blowing holes

I never blew a hole in a mountain to let a train through, but I did climb one—Medicine Bow Mountain, all of 12,000 feet. And I did fall in love with the mountains. Growing up in Cincinnati, hills were a necessary part of any beautiful landscape. And the neighboring Appalachians were just larger hills. But the mountains! Surprisingly, the first ones I saw were the Alps, driving from the north towards them, mere bumps on the horizon. Then the Zugspitz! Razor rocky craig mountain of my dream. Then the Rockies from New Mexico into Canada. Glorious! But the mantra mountain of my mind is Ruby Mountain, a low, tree covered mountain that just happens to reflect in Lake Diablo. It is in Washington in the Cascades, and I sat before it on three different camping trips for 29 days. It took that long to burn it ineffably, unutterably in my mind. I can just say or picture "Ruby Mountain," and peace comes. As I was writing the name, a relaxing breath much like a sigh carried my stress right out with it.

Living now in the Northwest, the mighty mother mountain Rainier tries unsuccessfully to bury Ruby in her glaciers. It can't, but I love the struggle--and the jealousy.

Find your mountain. Find your place. It is a life blessing.

One formerly brilliant image in my mind and reflecting glory to our country has become a faded, sad image. In 1974 I visited Glacier National Park and drove and walked deliriously among the toes of glaciers. I have pictures of white beauty which are now bare rock where once the sweet ice lay. Since Glacier was declared a park, 123 of its glaciers have vanished: from 150 to 27. (That stat comes from *This Moment on Earth* by the Kerrys, a book for White Outs like me who are more intellectual than natural. *A Moment* has a lot of momentous moments, researched facts, and is a little dry in the reading--John should have turned Teresa loose in this book to let her fill it with vinegar and invectives and then, like me, she could have sent it off before her spouse saw it).

150 glaciers shrunk to 27! And all of them, I repeat, all of them are projected to be gone in fifteen more years. Just as Chestnut Lane and Elm Boulevard will need to be renamed Asphalt Lane and Concrete Boulevard, so too, sadly, we must now rename Glacier National Park. Candidates? My two shots are *Bare Rocks*, and *Naked Mountains*—if those are too sexy, then *Moraines Remains*.

Since we can't count on a CO_2 reversal for decades to centuries, glacier officials had better learn from Austria and Switzerland, and soon France, and place a tarp over their glaciers. Otherwise I suggest the name change.

We've blown holes all over the earth, how about a hole in space if that were possible?

International idiots!

In 2007, I do not lie—a Russian astronaut drove a golf ball out of the loading dock from the international space station.

Just your usual unman.

The space station is moving about 7.7 km per second, so even with a hell of a hit in the opposite direction, that damn golf ball is now moving at 7.7 km per second.

Unfortunately these space stations are not all going in one nice direction. When race cars bump into each other, the relative collision speed isn't too bad because they are all going in the same direction. No sweat, and the driver usually steps out of the car. But you can't lose a tire in space, because some of the satellites go in retrograde orbits, counter to the spin of the earth. Now you've got 7.7 + 7.7 or a goddamngolfball coming at you faster than 15 km a second.

That'll go through you like you were a hologram. And you can't step out of that wreck. Fore!

But hey, it's just one more piece of space junk. Why make such a big deal out of a little ball? It's the parallel: what we've done to the land, to the ocean, we are doing to our neighboring space. And though there is a lot of room out there to pollute, we are on our way: NASA tracks about 500,000 of these pieces. Okay, some of them are small, but their average speed is 4 or 5 times the speed of a 22 bullet. No sweat. Fore! And that half million is a fraction of the total number. How did we put it all up there? For one example, the discarded upper stages of rockets, pressurized and still containing some fuel, eventually blow up and spew hundreds of thousands of untracked pieces. If you don't believe me, count 'em.

So hey, what's one golf ball added to the space junk diaspora. At least the golf ball's round so it will make a clean, smooth (probably not symmetrical) hole through you. And besides, a Russian drove the golf ball, and NASA in 2004 said Russia was the number one contributor to space junk. (Guess whose number 2?) So, from our pesticided, almost herbicided, monograssified fare way, Tiger can point his fingers right at the Russians and accuse them of taking a mulligan. But since a Canadian firm paid the Russians to hit the golf ball, that makes it all right, giving it an international blessing.

When we fill earth's space full of flying junk, there is always the rest of the universe. Do you realize how much time that daunting task gives us to stop polluting? But we need not concern ourselves with the energy costs and time to pollute deep space, before we get that far the unpleasant solution is much closer, right down here on earth, directly in front of us.

Bridge Out. Come on Kirby, get serious. Get your head out of space and your feet on the ground. Can't we see the yawning, gaping, huge, swallowing, abyssful end of civilization right in front of us? Why watch out for flying golf balls in space when we can drive right on in.

Okay, you want something serious? In the U.S each year 200,000 to 400,000 babies, while still in the uterus, have been exposed to enough mercury to cause nerve damage according to the National Health and Nutrition Examination Survey (NYT 4/26/07).

Last year those babies were born injured. This year other great big bundles of what should be joy are being born that way. They are our children. And we wonder about the dumbing down of America? It is because we are either too damn dumb or too lazy or too selfish to do anything about it.

How dumb are we?

Who do you think might grace the hood ornament of Grand Civil, the first into the future and the gulf? There are a lot of candidates, so let's select an unexpected one from our most dynamic scientific area.

Try the unmen biologists, the unbios who don't know what *bios* means, and who sell their knowledge of life to the perpetrators of death. Besides the terminal gene of ADM, they have re-created the polio virus, the 1918 killer flu virus, and now, out of our very DNA, parts of an old infectious retrovirus have been re-strung together to create the Phoenix virus! (*Discover* 2/07). I ask the unbios, do we not deserve self-extinction? And when you wipe us clean taking many life forms with us, could you please make an exception for the rats—they are of a nobler species than you, the unbios.

Isn't it easy to be sarcastic at such stupidity? Let me demonstrate again: Unbios, could you search for the gene of the serial killers and mass murderers, and combine the genes of those two types? First, though, take out a large life insurance policy on yourselves, the beneficiary being the life science of your choice.

Harder to be positive, but please, please biologists, as you reach your dendrites into the molecules of life, please go with nature, please go with life. Only after long-term thinking, please tease carefully those ancient, sacred, strands of life.

And do not rationalize that whatever you do is right with this argument: *humans are part of nature and therefore it is natural for us to step out of nature.* Don't give me that twisted pap that because we big-brained builders and destroyers are products of nature, therefore all we do, all we create and destroy, is natural—therefore we can do what the hell we please.

It's just the opposite—insects bound by genetic programming can do what the hell they please (except mosquitoes concerning which I am a perverted deviant), because that is what they must do.

Higher forms of animals learn—a wolf meets a skunk or a porcupine and learns it cannot do whatever the hell it pleases without a smelly or painful consequence.

And us? While all things natural are good, all things natural are not necessarily good for us—it depends upon time and place and use: arsenic used as a condiment, or an active volcano used as a foot warmer, are not good for us, but they are good for the earth.

Arsenic is an essential trace element in some animals, and perhaps in humans. Essential. Without it, those animals die.

In its natural locations, arsenic is widely spread across the earth, and is usually fairly diluted and safe—until: mining, draining of lakes, pesticides, factories, and furnaces place much of the arsenic in the air. Unmen place about 17 times the arsenic in the air as do natural things, such as our toasty volcano.

And once in the air, we cannot filter the entire atmosphere--so go outside, or inside, at your own risk. We breathe it, the plants absorb it, the fish bioaccumulate it, and we eat the arsenic.

And pray tell, what good is this fiery foot toaster? Volcanoes simply give us the ground to stand on. As the magma wells up from the pacific floor, it spreads the tectonic plates we stand upon. Our earth. Thank you volcanoes. Who in the hell cares about Hawaii anyhow?

Now don't ask me to defend the earth's right to hurricanes and earthquakes and tsunamis and so forth. It's just there. Deal with it. It's our earth. And if Yellowstone's gigantic caldera decides to blow, we will never plug it. We accept it. Just move west fast young man, far west.

We can do something, however, about putting more arsenic in the air, and also do something about the growing unmentionable. We can sneak a peek at the last chapter, and maybe start putting the brakes on Civil.

Two eye-boggling eyesores: when I was camping near the Sawtooth mountains, and had hiked up to where no one had gone before, I found a small pine tree that some sub-unman had hung with beer bottles, cans, wine bottles, and booze bottles. Perhaps it was in a drunken blur. Perhaps it was teenagers displaying the only rite of passage our society offers them. Perhaps it was a protest to pollution. But whatever, it replaced my best memory of my best Christmas tree. Unreal. History? Or prophecy.

On a high bank overlooking Lake Michigan, I saw an even uglier sight three years ago that is still there— plastic bags of dog shit hanging high in the trees. People scoop their dog droppings into plastic bags and then hurl the bags of excrement from the top of the bank into the trees below. Some catch on the branches and hang there.

They are unreachable even by a fire engine bucket.
Grooooss.

Far better to have left the poop on the sidewalk,
stepped in it, and then wiped it on their carpets back in their
homes. And do we blame the dogs or the humans?

Do we need any better example of which animal is
messing up earth more? Which animal would the world be
better off without? If you were the chief species
extinguisher (and you are) and you could push one button
and extinguish one species for the good of the planet,
which button would you push?

I don't want to start an international war, but we
could ask that same question about countries.

Gibran said that butterflies will hover when
pyramids are leveled—he's wrong about butterflies, but he's
right about life. Species zap out of existence. Life doesn't.
But Sandburg was right about the grass taking over
vanished civilization.

Right now we are busily zapping species, probably
more than half of all species in our lifetime. We are one of
the six greatest life-extinguishing mass catastrophes—and
the butterflies are not doing so well. I know. While I have
not gone down to their Mexico migration forest and
counted the monarchs, I have read they are thinning.
Butterfly counts show the entire population down about
40% over the last 20 years. That's a lot of missing pieces of
floating beauty.

I know from my experience and you do too that
they are fluttering away. Think of the butterflies you saw in
your youth. And I am not being a romantic here that
everything in our youth was bright and beautiful, but think
of the fields full of flowers and butterflies. And now, if you
can find fields, try to find the butterflies. In the last ten
years I have seen only six, (6) species. I have counted. I
don't know their names, but they are fairly distinctively
colored. And if you don't believe me, you start counting.

Okay, Der, it's not you and I. Not directly anyway. We are not taking fly swatters to butterflies. But Civil is. Look at the windshield. And look at the exhaust felling them like autumn leaves. But we ride in Civil. So indirectly, yeh, you and I are killing a bunch. And you would think that Pandora, being a lady, would like butterflies. She doesn't. She eats them in her salads. There won't be many greens left soon, or butterflies, so eat up now.

Please allow me a poetic digression and the poetic license to use a little hyperbole in the last line. Enjoy:

a flash
a flutter
a shock

a yellowgoldenbutterfly!

not seen since youth
when fluttering skies
were full of yellows
floating like autumn leaves

shock--a sole flutterer

where have the butterflies gone?
the snows of yesteryear return

spring summer fall returns
but no floating butterflies

have we acidified the air
burning their butter powder
from the wings
of these frail fliers

once like stars in the sky
now a lone flash
and ghostly gone
a fading memory
my children will never know

we, no I too, have killed
the last butterfly

Life will outlast Unmen. We as a species, as sure as 99% of all former species, will be zapped.

Only difference, we are zapping ourselves.

Zap out enough species, and ZAP! There goes unman.

If you would prefer me to say that more elegantly, try this: In the long line of life, almost all species blink and are gone. Only the humans blink themselves.

And if the rest of the species could talk, they would say: "Good riddance!" I have already posed the question to us humans: who is the most dangerous species. If the species could cast a vote on this issue, it would be an almost universal vote of 1.9 million species to 3 selecting the Unmen as most dangerous. Dogs, cats, and rats would vote for us.

Don't you feel weird walking in a room of strangers, and worse in a room of enemies?

Don't you feel bad when the world hates America because of Iraq and Guantanamo?

Don't you feel awful, (well you should—I don't, because I have not thought about it to this point) walking in a forest of life, knowing you are public, world, and life enemy number one?

We are a walking death stick.

With or without a gun.

If we think of comparisons, say, for the most dangerous, terrible humans--Hitler and Stalin rise to the top. If we think of the most dangerous, terrible species--we are the top.

And I admit my membership to that dangerous species, for I waste a lot. Last Thanksgiving we had 14 bags of refuse. I can start my usual rationalizing again, like I did with my van, by saying our entire family was home meeting my first granddaughter, and that we were celebrating Christmas early—thus the amount. And I could brag that ten of the bags were separated for recycling—but all those words do not justify those other four giant black plastic bags heading for the landfill. How much of those four could have been composted?

Some of my good friends, deeper within the city than I, compost. I will compost someday. Ouch. Another potentially broken daydream. But I will compost with my body, at least after I pollute the air and give my ashes to...And the contents of those plastic bags could have been placed in garbage cans or biodegradable brown paper bags and dumped into the truck instead of being wrapped in plastic.

I'm feeling guilty now, but guilt is good.

I can do better—I realized that as I peeled a banana for cereal. I tossed the peel into a black plastic bag. But notice the heroism. I have confessed my crime, unlike the Bush White House Administration "misplacing" millions of e-mails, I could have said with them: "I *misplaced* my banana peel." *Mis* is now the hot word of holy pardon. What else can we do with it? I mistook my bribe. I misfucked my affair. And sorry honey, but I misforgot our wedding anniversary. And don't forget, I mis-hit the little ole lady crossing the street. I'm innocent.

Damn we unmen can sure talk purty. We sure hide dirty. Those 4 bags--I miscycled them.

But if I would reduce those four bags to two, and you would also, we would abolish half of the landfills! And if we sacked the plastic sacks, the rest of our garbage would biodegrade more quickly. So stick your hand in and pull out those coffee grounds and shake your fingers into the compost--and I'll get my wife to do likewise. I tried hard this week and I got the garbage down to one small white bag. (Don't ask how often I ate out, or of what material the white bag was made of.)

After that verbal dog and phony show—some serious words from the sea. Krill is down 80% or so in the last 30 years, probably because of the unmentionable. But krill are so low on the food chain, so small, so what? They are low on the chain, and that is the problem: they are foundational. Pull a block from the bottom of a stack, and what happens to us, the blocks at the top of the food chain?

And while we're in deep water without a krill to stand on, would you believe that a bio firm took a gene from a carp, grew it in a safflower, and put it into a shrimp to bolster its immunity system. That was a quickie. And sometimes our unbios should do a little trans hygiene genetic history before we misfuck life forms. Evolution took a long time to mix your genes into beautiful you—and

I know you are beautiful, because all four of my readers are.

I have seen enough monster movies that screwing with genes scares the hell out of me. I believe in freedom, but jesuschristmosesmohammedbuddhaandtherest, can't their community of peers police them? After our industrial-chemical-nuclear insults, do we have to add biological? I am not against any of that litany of four, just the uncontrolled, polluting use by the unmen.

Oceans are big—too big for me, but when The Marine Stewardship Council, a British group, has to certify a fishery as sustainable, I want to drown. Earlier I glanced at the scenario of the Gulf Stream flow stopping and Europe freezing. And our coral reefs? Home to our greatest biodiversity.

Let us sit upon the waves and weep salt tears for the death of things.

In the 1970s we got serious about ozone, and have held the hole in check. When science showed that CFCs released chlorine atoms into the stratosphere which rip up the ozone, we banned those products. We believed science.

Now when it comes to the unmentionable, we don't even need science. Heck, just sit in your car in the summer with the windows up—greenhouse. When it's that simple, why don't we believe science?

But if you want another, simpler, visualizable science, picture this: ice in Greenland and Antarctica forms annual layers of freeze/melt which allows us to count the past years just like tree rings. Inside that ice are tiny bubbles of CO_2. Guess what? As Grand Civil started rolling, the bubbles started blowing. The faster Grand rolled, the greater the concentration of CO_2. As Grand Civil rattled its hood and really roared, the bubbles swelled up in a straight line progression! Never turning downward. Year after year. Strong correlative proof.

And if that is not good enough for you, while you're in your car in the sun, keep the windows up and enjoy the greenhouse effect--and while you're toasty, try to sniff a bubble or two if you can.

Has our technology penetrated everywhere? From the oceans to the top of the world where oxygen tanks and blue and orange mountain gear litters Mt. Everest. From ocean bottom to mountain top, where can I find the pre-unman garden. Twice I tried to escape the steel talons of technology. I backpacked alone into a National Forest, walked off the path till it got dark, and I pitched my tent— at that time it was more a macho thing to conquer fear than to step outside of technology. I did not sleep, for large foot steps followed by snorts just outside my thin tent wall kept jackknifing me into a crouching position, ready to fight the bear with my bowie knife, (Jim Bowie, Davy Crockett style). When dawn filtered in, I went out to void my fears, and saw that I had planted my tent in a deer path! I fell back to sleep, finally at peace in the garden of eden but then, worse than all the snorts and breaking twigs, an unbeastly mechanical roar! Ripping up the ravines came the unman on a motorcycle.

I'm glad I did not have a gun. I would have shot, not to hit, probably not even to take out the tires, but just to scare the shit out of his head. I would have been wrong, of course. He had just as much right as I did to the woods— well, just as much legal unman right, but far from a moral, natural right.

I won't digress into an ethic, or I will become a preacher instead of a passenger caught in the car of civilization with you, a car too big to even get near the doors, impossible to climb over the thousands of unmen sitting in the rows of seats around us. And can we even dream about clawing our way to the front giant seat to feebly put our tiny feet on the brake when millions and billions of others press down hard upon the gas pedal. Pedal to the metal. Full speed ahead. Bridge Out.

On a second attempt to escape technology, I backpacked with my son into the Allegheny National Forest, six hour's walk away from the closest road. To be honest, I was trying more to bond with my son than to break the pinching pliers of Pandora. We pitched a tent high overlooking a lake; and in this place of utopian peace, a boat of drunken revelers yelling and whooping came full-throttle into the cove below us. My face burned red. Where is that gun? Another camper took defensive action: he had a few fourth of July rockets with him, which he angled down at the boat and fired. The boat wheeled about. I cheered.

I didn't care that tech had battled tech, even though at that time I thought technology could not heal itself. It still can't. No more than a computer can think and run the world. The unmen can't either, since they have let tech run amok, even while appearing so marvelous and wonderful. But humans can help to heal. They can control the power and the glory of human inventions by *adding to* nature, not destroying it. Humans can, since they make and run technology—at least theoretically they can control technology. The unmen can't, but the humans can: *physician heal thyself.* Keep your instruments, humans, but quit using dirty needles, and the world will grow healthier.

It happened. I have just discovered it while writing this book! I now see a way, if unmen can become human, a way that we can retain much of our culture while stopping the great hurt we are putting on earth—and on ourselves. We can stop Civil. And no, it is not one of my sarcastic jokes this time with the solution something like: blow the damn thing up.

I've got it! I've really got it! It's a hope and a path towards a harmony of tech with nature. It's doable! If you help me.

I will hold that hope until later in the book because I'm too lazy to change all my nasty words; and I'm having fun because it is a lot easier to curse than create, to break than to build; so I will continue on my sardonic way, and we will have to wait for salvation.

So—who bears the guilt here? It started with Thomas Newcomen in 1712 when he invented the steam engine. I am indebted (and jealous too) of Bill McKibben's excellent ironical insight: Newcomen burnt coal to pump water out of a coal mine in order to get more coal. The stored energy of the earth was used against the earth to unleash tons and eons of stored energy to pour into our air and waters.

But Newcomen was just inventing without knowing. But what of the mining, tobacco, oil, and chemical companies who knew. They knew about Love Canal and Hooker and Hanford. Almost with the certainty of Nazi doctors, they knew. It was easier for them to live with their knowing than the Nazi doctors, for their hands did not reach into living flesh and destroy it. Once removed from the dying, it becomes a white collar crime. A white collar with grime and blood on the inside of the collar. The hypocritical white collar, hiding black death in the world. You can be sure the driver of Grand Civil Supreme has had, and has, the current symbolic equivalent of a white collar.

Father, don't forgive that white collar killer.

And probably don't forgive me, for I have hate in my heart.

If two of my buddies didn't own filling stations, and if I didn't have the black petrol blood on my hands, I would suggest to every male to use the pumps like dogs use fire plugs. And females go for it too—just don't hurt yourself.

As you pass the pumps, mentally pee on them. Later that image might help us stay on the road, brake, turn, and steer towards sanity.

One of the latest schemes to burn my behind, as the globe continues to heat up, is: buy carbon credits. So, pollute and pay for it! Does that sound okay? Hell, crap all over and then pay someone to clean it up? Why not stop the ubiquitous crapping, since you are crapping not only in your back yard, but on the earth, which is our backyard. NIMBY! (I didn't use to like that acronym until just now, when it was properly applied.) Is it okay for a smoker to blow smoke in your face and say, "Don't worry, I'm buying filter credits." Bullshit, smokeshit, rationalizationshit, hypocrisy, bribery! You cannot pay for your excursion outside our global morality.

Let me tell you what that is like. As a little Catholic I used to sin and go to confession; then I could go right out and sin again cause I could wipe my carbon sins away by saying three Hail Marys.

Do you believe that? If so, the pope wants you! So pay about $28 extra for a plane ticket so you can spew over a ton of CO_2 in the air, and then spew it again for another $28 bucks.

So go ahead, screw the ho and toss Madam Pandora another $20 so you can carbon screw her again next week!

Instead—here's another plan. Just be big and admit that you are polluting. And then do something about it: pollute less; push Congress for a different energy source; separate the sin from the reparation; separate the pollution from the carbon credits; then, in a *separate* act, go ahead and plant trees. And pay to plant them. And buy rainforests and conservation land. That's great. But don't salve your stinking smoking conscience by saying now you can live in a mansion, and fly your private air liners over our backyards, because you have paid for it. In 2015, 1700 private jets flew to Davos, Switzerland, to the World Economic Forum to discuss climate change and economic inequality. Relish and curse the double irony.

NIMBY.

Not you.

Not anyone.

No one has the right to pollute the air, the water, or the land which belong to all life forms.

How's your pee? (The following stats on your excretory functions are lifted from Physicians for Social Responsibility (at www.oregonpsr.org). Urine samples from over 1,000 adults showed that over one-half of them had 6 or more pesticides in their pee.

Since most of those thousand plus adults had not recently sprayed for cockroaches—that means they had been carrying the pesticides inside themselves and were gradually excreting them. Since odds are good you too, Der, have six or more, I suggest you pee now, if you have any left over from dogging the gas pumps as suggested above, and *carry your water to the wise woman*--wasn't I nice and polite to use Shakespearean language.

Where did those pesticides come from? Bad news-- 90% of our streams sampled had pesticides, and streams are usually considered purer than rivers; but good news--only 50% of the wells sampled had pesticides.

So what do we do? Quit inhaling, eating, and drinking, and you won't build up your pesticide reservoir.

For all our medical marvels, we have been slow on this pee thing. The Greeks tasted the sweetness of urine to diagnose diabetes, and Shakespeare used a wise woman. So why wasn't it until 1993 that the National Academy of Science reported pesticides in the diets of children? Once they got peeing, then they actually began looking at the pesticides in babies, then fetuses, then pregnant women, then women of childbearing age, then all women. (What about us, guys, huh? We make babies, too). And looking at that progression, your guess is right—stunningly the pesticides were in all five ages of life. All of them.

That means you, Der. Sorry to inform you.
And me, even though I was not tested, I now know why the flowers in the back yard died.

And mothers? Breast milk has been analyzed that contains PCBs, pesticides, dioxin, dibenzofurans, flame retardants (at least the baby won't burn as she/he nurses), lead, and mercury—one-sixth of the mothers had harmful levels of mercury, and phthalates from cosmetics.

Finally, in 1996, Congress ordered the EPA to protect children. In 2001, the Center for Disease Control used biomonitoring to test levels of 27 chemicals in blood and urine samples. Slowly we were getting to get there: 27 chemicals tested, only 4,234 to go. But cheer up, the CDC does have a National Biomonitoring Program that, as of 2015, has a pilot program going (repeat--only a *pilot*) that is testing about 100 nutritional indicators and chemicals in infants and pregnant women. We've arrived! 100 tested, only 4,134 to go.

Now, if you want to stretch your brain, try to comprehend 92 million organic and inorganic substances and 65 million sequences that are listed in the CAS Registry (Chemical Abstract Services), a division of the American Chemical Society. 157 million!!?? But you had better check that number quickly, because it grows by about 15,000 a day! (I'm running out of exclamation points, so please pause and consider that...) So where is the evil source of these poisons in our mothers' milk and babies bodies? Pandora's pits, brewing unnatural compounds never found in nature, spewing billions of pounds into the air, throwing millions of pounds of older, well-known killer carcinogens such as PCB, alcohol, lead, mercury dioxin, and cadmium.

Hard to believe you and I would allow that. Then who are these unmen minions of Pandora? Answer: who owns the factories? Who are the corporate heads? Who buys the products? And who drives the cars?

In about 1952, the last pure air in the U.S. disappeared. The passing was mourned and measured at 2,000 particulates per some unit, probably cc, at Flagstaff Arizona. (Don't be a *but* person, and say why didn't they measure it in Alaska. I'd then have to *but* back and say Alaska wasn't a state then. (Love that Wikipedia, and it's getting more scholarly, but still, *caveat lector*).

Good thing they didn't measure air pollution in Cincy in 1952. They might have needed a scale. I remember soot falling like snowflakes from the sky. Was Dad burning that cheap bituminous instead of the harder anthracite? I just remember closing my eyes, putting my head down, and feeling yuk. Fifty years later my son would go to China and describe soot filled cities. That was before the Beijing Olympics. Since then our power/pollution appetite has spread. The world has caught the fever, and the long term prognostication—temperature rising, fever fatal. (Oblique references to glowwarm do not count).

My first air pollution warning didn't come until 1969. I stood in my office on the 21st floor at the UI at Chicago overlooking the massive Chicago cloverleaf of the Edens, the Ryan, and the Eisenhower. Below me was a tennis court that I used to play on. If I hit a ball over the fence, it would be popped by a car tire like we pop bubble wrap. I quit playing on that court not because my salary wouldn't pay for lost balls, but because of ozone warnings saying it was unsafe to exercise outdoors. Unsafe to exercise? To breathe a lot?

Ozone should have awakened me and the world right then. But it didn't. I couldn't smell the ozone like some claimed, but I did see it—I saw my first smog from an airplane descending into Chicago in the early seventies. A wafer of grey yellow spread over the entire city. I watched my plane sink into it, settle on O'Hare's runway, and my breath felt smothered. I'm sure it was all psychological. But the smog wasn't. I knew it was there.

But even more scary, when I stood outside and looked up, I could see nothing but blue sky. I was astonished because I was looking right through maybe a half mile of pollution, and I could not see it. I had needed the perspective of the plane's window to look through it horizontally, through the pancake shape fifty or so miles across. I felt creepy. I was breathing something that I knew was there but I couldn't see it! I was breathing pollution! So was everyone else, and they didn't know it either. Our whole city sky was polluted, but my eyes automatically adjusted to the duller color of the blue and did not see the smog. Yuk! And I still shiver recalling it. And last summer it hung over Denver, and again I shuddered, but what the heck, I'm getting used to it; besides, it's comfy in Grand Civil. What do you want me to do? I can't pinch my nose and stop breathing.

Over our other cities the mess we are in rears its smoky fangs, and smiles. I had been blissfully unaware that smog had been a problem in L.A. back in the fifties. Why hadn't our world seen it then? As I told you, I had seen it as a child in the form of soot settling over Cincinnati, and I closed my eyes, but I hadn't connected it to all the air over our earth. I had merely connected it to our coal-fired furnaces. That backyard soot-filled sky of my youth is no longer childish--it is greedy, it is wrong, it is deadly, it is earth defying, life defying. And we who do it are killers of the skies. We slice it like a ninja with the invisible knives of arsenic and mercury and other unseen blades.

Most of those chemicals are not tested for harm, and even less likely are they tested for reproductive toxicity. If 76% of people have pyrethroid insecticides in their system, what does not mean? And what about acrolen, bernzine, benzolalpyrene, bisphenol-A, brominated flame retardants (BERs), diesel, formaldehyde, phthalates (those are in a lot of body care products—and watch out men, they might screw with your screwing apparatus) , paraquat, dieldrin, maneb, mancozeb, MPTP…. And 157,000,000 others? Do you know industrial males have half the sperm count of primitive societies?

And children? 92% of a Minnesota sample had residues of chlorpyrifos metabolite in them.

DES, a synthetic estrogen now banned, raised a new born girl's chances of getting cancer by forty times (that's right, 40). A former colleague of mine, whose daughter had cancer, saved her pharmaceutical bills and became a key witness in a lawsuit against those manufacturers.

If those big chemical names and large percentages are too much to think about, because we don't want to think about them because, helplessly, we have to breathe, then inhale the list below. Unmen are exhaling these chemicals right into your lungs. Here are some just from the alphabetical "B" list of chemicals from a very old list:

Benzoic Acid
Benzoin
Benzaldehyde
Benzyl Alcohol
Benzophenone
Benzaldehyde Glycerol Acetal
Benzyl Benzoate
Benzyl Butyrate
Benzyl Cinnamate
Benzyl Propionate
Benzyl Salicylate
Butyric Acid
Bisabolene
Borneol
Bornyl Acetate
1,3-Butanediol
2,3-Butanedione
1-Butanol
2-Butanone
Butyl Acetate

Butyl Butyrate
Butyl Isovalerate
Butyl Undecylenate
Butylidenephthalide
4-(2-Butenylidene)-3,5,5-Trimethyl-2-Cyclohexen-
1-One

Whew! Inhale that last one. Those B-chemicals that you've been sniffing are from a 1994 *government approved* [sic] list that allows 599 additives in cigarettes. I don't know most of those chemicals, but they don't sound very lung friendly. And those are just from cigarettes.

Time for a quick break for a lesser insult to our living earth—noise pollution. It disrupts the territorial habits of birds, and thus their breeding. Noise pollution disrupts breeding?

And what's in those healthy fruits and vegetables? At least 1 pesticide is found in 72% of those oh-so-good-for-you fruits.

If you prefer your fruits or nuts prepared for you in those nice plastic containers, you had better turn them upside down first. I just finished some sunflower seeds, rinsed the container, and freaked out. Number 3 was written in that neat little equilateral triangle on the *inside* bottom. Number three is polyvinyl chloride! The Center for Environment, Health and Justice calls PVC "The Poison Plastic." Children's Health Environmental Coalition calls it "The Most Toxic Plastic." Help! I've been poisoned! And I don't think the sunflower seeds saved me.

Make sure you don't die before you buy--flip the container upside down and read the number on the bottom (since my poisonous container was stamped on the inside, you might be reading the number backwards). There are three (3) very bad numbers. You can remember because the first is 3. Then the second two add up to 13, the unlucky number. So don't eat out of 3, 6 or 7. When you see these numbers in the triangle, mentally superimpose the skull and crossbones upon them and yell for the manager. Shout out that the store is poisoning its customers. You will get attention.

Probably avoid numbers 4 and 5, but don't yell at the manager. And a cute little rhyme, compliments of your author: "1 & 2, okay for you; 4 and 5 you'll stay alive." Eat only out of grandma's glass Ball and Mason jars. My lovely wife, who will never read my tirades will miss her praise here: she just replaced all the plastic with glass storage containers. Into the fridge, into the microwave, and into your mouth with no poison plastic.

Okay, poisons are all over, but not in our house, right? Oh yeh? The average home had 10 to 100 times higher air pollution concentrations than the outside.

What the hell have we done with our air, our water, our land, our home?

We know nature has its own natural poisonous defenses in snakes, plants, and a few toads. But when did the last friend you know die from a snake bite? Or by touching a toad? Or even by eating a poisonous mushroom?

But some of your friends are dead, right? So who tells you what toxins took out your last friend? Toxins are there--everywhere. A survey of about 700 women of childbearing age from rural and urban America, found an average of 145 toxins in the bodies of those women. And the placenta allows too many of those poisons to pass right into their child in their womb. I'm still looking for that research article, but other research is coming in that will make that small sample of 700 seem irrelevant. In 2007 Alberta Canada is testing the domestic and industrial toxins found in the blood of 30,000 pregnant women. I can't wait; for the results to be released. But I think I'll have to, for it is 2015 and I can't find them. Scary? You go, Canada!

Hold it. Not so fast, O Canada. Canadian industries are required to lower glowwarm by 18% over three years.

Dove. But that decrease is tied only to units of production, and not overall glowwarm output. Serpent. Result, emissions will probably rise rather than decrease, and Canada will be 13 years late in meeting its Kyoto commitment (NYT 4/27/07).

Beware the serpent folded in the dove's wings.

But, hey, let's not rip on Canada. How are we doing with our Kyoto commitment, Der? And being intelligent, you have asked, "What commitment?" Our scientists speak in unified voice, but they are not heard. have called for a mild reduction in greenhouse gas. I call that, a pale shade of green. And your poetic lesson that money speaks louder than knowledge:

> When scientists speak
> sounds like a mouse's squeak.
> When corporate spreads green
> It's heard like a scream.

Quote that at your next board meeting.

I know some of us, even those without child-carrying capacity plus 145 poisons, are getting freaked out, but this next superficial item might entangle some deeper emotions than mere motherhood--it concerns the crowning glory of women: The National Academy of Science set a benchmark of 12 parts per billion of mercury concentration in a woman's hair.

In a woman's hair? At least the uterus doesn't show on the outside, and besides, the danger's in the future, but hair! I'll bet that'll get some babes pissed at Pandora. And some men too. I love hair. If I nibble on my lover's locks, will my brain dissolve in a silver-grey pool? I don't care if it's only a small amount of mercury, it's there! It's a bad, bad, very bad hair day for humanity. It's a bad hair life. And these glittering mercury curls are symptomatic of the toxins that surround us—toxins we made.

I forgive you, Der, for having mercury in your hair. It wasn't your fault. But damn if I'm going to run my teeth through your hair. And I'm thinking twice about even running my fingers.

If you think I lost it to the devil in the details, then just google *poisons in pregnant women* and savor the five million hits!

Damn!

But why rip on women? Men, this one will hit you where it hurts. It's a study on rats.

Who cares about rats?

But it's a study on the rats' testes and sperm count. Now it's getting a little more interesting.

Pesticides cause rats to have smaller balls.

Poor rats.

But this study applies to you, man.

Now you've got my attention! You hit me in the nuts.

Good, because pesticides can cause your sons to have smaller balls which means less sperm which deletes your unconceived grandchildren. Maybe that's part of the 50% less sperm that you have than those natives who live in non-pesticided, remote areas.

You've erected my male interest. Give me the bio details.

Professor Skinner in Washington State found that a common pesticide, methoxychlor, and a fungicide, vinclozin disrupted methyl groups on the DNA. These methyl groups activate genes and the rat pups had fewer sperm, slower sperm, and more dead sperm.

Ouch!

Hang on. It gets worse, but you asked for the bio details. But it could get better if you take actions.

The poisons of the parents are visited upon the children: a Seattle paper reported some scary rat results: those same two pesticides, vinclozin (helps keep the fungus out of your wines) and methoxychlor (kills bugs) attached a methyl group to the DNA which was passed onto the rat litter. "In human terms, this would mean if your great grandmother was exposed to an environmental toxin at a critical point in her pregnancy, you may have inherited the disease" (SPI 6/3/05). But not to worry—so far the study has only been done on rats, and we men, cruising in Civil, are beyond mere rats, and by our actions, beyond nature itself.

So avoid having grandmothers who are exposed to vinclozin and methoxychlor. And remember, what ain't good for rats ain't good for you, man. Nor your children. Feel desperate? Good. Then stop laughing at women who are worried about mercury in their hair. And respect the rats, and all living creatures from bacteria to the blue whale. Except mosquitoes. Swat 'em. And do something. Don't pass an injured earth and smaller balls down to your kids.

Did Gram know what she was doing when she walked the green curving rows of the vineyard, inhaling the promise of joy, and imbibing the fruit of our vines?

Of course not, so we've already forgiven our Grams and Gramps and Moms and Dads for not knowing.

The last dolphin died. Really. If your mercury laced hair didn't twinge you, that one will. Dolphins swim as sinuously, as lovely as long, swirling hair. But in the interest of maintaining my cover as a truthteller, let me *qualify* that dolphin statement: the last *white river* dolphin died.

That's true. I read it in the NYT: the white river dolphin of the Yangtze River is "functionally extinct." In 1997 a search found 13 white river dolphins. In 2006, a six-week search found none. Maybe there are a few the searching crew missed. Can you picture the last lonely dolphin looking for a mate? Thank you China, one of our old civilizations

Would you have paid any attention if I said that the last baiji died? (That is the name of the species.) Of course not, but dolphins are close to our hearts. We love them--big friendly playful intelligent huggable mammals—huggable, that's the thing! Every girl's dream to swim with the dolphins. (And I confess, mine too, so I guess it is not a sexual thing. Reserve your crude comments to yourself).

Well, we can blame China for killing them. After all, how could a white dolphin swim in the Yangtze and the Yellow River (excuse me, all Chinese rivers look alive, the Huang He). I am not racist here, because I was really yellow once when I was jaundiced. We are actually color blind, not seeing the real colors. As one of my "black" students said to me: "I'm not black, I'm brown. And you're pink."

Who are you calling a pinko? Don't you care about your grade?

How can we blame China for the death of the baiji when we did the same thing a long time ago—back in the 1950s we killed the last monk seal, right in the Caribbean.

Dolphins and seals, I appeal to you as intelligent species. Learn from the baiji and monk seals. Just because the image of Civil in this book is that of a land monster, don't think you are safe. If we don't fish you to death, we'll get you through the oil flowing into our sewers, and the poisons in the air which rain on your waters. It all runs together. Your lives and ours. Civil sends its gift to you, too, dolphins and seals and all creatures of the sea. And the gift returns to us.

Sometimes we pay attention when the large mammals, creatures closer to us like the dolphins and the seals, become extinct. But small as well as large life is winking out all around us. We are in the sixth greatest mass extinction since life began on earth. And it's not volcanoes or meteors causing it. It's us! The unmen. Hop in civil and let's smash some more. If that doesn't scare you, simply consider that all the species alive on earth did not exist at one time (please except some of those earliest life forms like the protista, the archae, and some bacteria). That means that the predecessors of all the species that you can see with your eyes no longer exist. To simplify, let's just say they died and apply Aristotelian syllogistic logic:

Major premise: All species die.
Minor premise: We are a species.
Conclusion: Therefore we will die.

Not complicated. Four large questions remain: How will it happen? When will it happen? How fast will we speed up our own end? And the major question of this book—what are we going to do about it?

Are we a suicidal species? I don't think so.

It's just that for all our big brains, we think small. We think mainly of the immediate. Although we can read shallowly into the past, and project shadowy into the future, we don't often use those skills. We are greedy want-it-all-now-animals. Eat it all, and the hell with the children to come.

Beware all animals. Beware our children. Microbe to mammal, you cannot swim, run, or fly away from us; we are life's crest and creation, we, the most intelligent mammal of them all!

All dolphins, bow your heads. All mammals kneel in comrade sympathy. All life pay your last respects and say your last funereal farewell to the last baiji. Farewell dolphin.

It's time for a poem to lighten this grief. The poet Hopkins watches a small girl mourning over autumn's leaves, and his conclusion is for all of us:

Margaret, are you grieving
Over Goldengrove unleaving?
Leaves, like the things of man, you
With your fresh thoughts care for, can you?
Ah! as the heart grows older
It will come to such sights colder
By and by, nor spare a sigh
Though worlds of wanwood leafmeal lie;
And yet you will weep and know why.
Now no matter, child, the name:
Sorrow's springs are the same.
Nor mouth had, no nor mind, expressed
What heart heard of, ghost guessed:
It is the blight man was born for,
It is Margaret you mourn for.

-- Gerard Manley Hopkins

We mourn for ourselves. When we were children
and knew not what we mourned for: for a world that was
vanishing under concrete and smog, for a deeper return to
the natural death of things. We were guiltless. No one
taught us. How could they? For our parents did not know
then what they were losing or how they were destroying it.

Environmentally, we are the evil empire. One of my
children called us that before we invaded Iraq on phony
pretenses, and he did not limit it to the environment. We
burn more energy, and therefore pollute more per person,
than any other nation, and about four times per person as
China. Kyoto? Come now. We wouldn't even agree to slow
our pollution though every other participating nation would
have agreed. Okay, so we don't like how other nations are
regulated, but negotiate, damn it. If you failed at One, start
a whole bunch of more Kyotos--and get serious. Slow the

pollution and the approaching unmentionable. And while you're at it, quit pushing the cigarettes and the coal into other countries.

But now that we know, is there any hope when our Grand Culture Supreme is in the hands of governments and corporations? Is there any hope when it hurtles with the terrible unturnable intensity of an asteroid of immense inertia, burning towards the bridge out sign which is becoming clearer and clearer, which we all can see, which we all can read; but pitifully few of us try to respond, and those who do so have well-intentioned but seemingly helpless movements like children flailing their arms.

Better to flail and fail, than not try and die.

I am sorry it took such ugly actions of our country against Kyoto, against the EPA, and against our earth—all in favor of oil and wealth, to cause me to spring so lately to life, for life. I would rather have flowed more naturally from the beauty and life of nature itself. But I'm here. And I'm pissed. And I hope you are pissed too.

Damn it. Where are our national priorities? Our health should be number one—and that is umbilically connected to the health of the air and water and earth. And our jobs should be number two, and all jobs should flow naturally from, and return to the earth. And all subsequent priorities should follow from life--for without life, there is nothing else.

And screw wars while you're at it. They don't belong on a national list of priorities. Our constitution reads to "provide for the common defense," not go kick someone's ass because we can. Or because they have oil. Or because they are a short cut across the Isthmus of Panama.

what can we do?

Have we learned anything in this Great White Out? Listen to Leopold:

We know now what was unknown to all the preceding caravan of generations: that men are only fellow-voyagers with other creatures in the odyssey of evolution. This new knowledge should have given us, by this time, a sense of kinship with fellow-creatures; a wish to live and let live; a sense of wonder over the magnitude and duration of the biotic enterprise.

Have we learned that we are not Kings and Queens over all creation, but "fellow-voyagers"? What can we do, oh generation of the Great White Out? What can we do as the caged awareness circles in our stomachs? What can we do for this earth before we leave it to our children?

We can at least seek for a way to slow down, if not stop Civil from reaching the bridge. We have read the sign, we see the signs, we must act. As we raise our awareness we must raise that of others. We must buy green, buy used, re-use, re-cycle, but that's not enough. We have to break the lock on oil, coal, and yes, even the returning nuclear. We must push for hydrogen, wind, solar, geothermal, and the biggest—read the last chapter of this book.

Or, we can pass the buck with a 'good luck' to our kids.

Hell, didn't our dads dump it on us? No, that's pure scapegoating, since they thought they were raining pure water down upon us, and handing us the magic of the machine. But now we know better. So Father forgive us if we dump it on our children, for we now know what we do.

A good beginning is with awareness. There is a green awakening. Is it in time? As a friend and poet puts it: *An Inch Before Too Late:*

Gaia:
vital cell

within mystical body
of living cosmos
but imperiled of late
by plundering human unkind
at last thankfully awakening
(as divine drama would have it)
an inch before too late.
                    Charles C. Finn

Since I am presenting myself as an open and honest man, I confess I have copied that poem without permission in violation of the copyright law. I didn't even tell my friend who will get a free copy (bribe) of this book and thus not sue me. You can find his other books on poetrybycharlescfinn.com That is a blatant advertisement because I love him. There, now he had better write a poem about me....on second thought, great poetry probes the mystery of the true, the good, and the beautiful—forget the poem, Charlie.

If we are in The Great White Out, an intellectual, reading community that understands the deep, long term, building problems, I probably should mention some books. But where to start? Back with the Greek Cynics who advocated the simple life in nature. Philosophically, they went into the hedonists, the epicureans, the romantics, the Beats, and the Hippies, and into us. There have been great books along the way, perhaps most pivotally being Muir and Leopold and you know the rest.

But since we can't change the world in a big way until we read the last chapter, what can we do in the interim before we dump our lives' mess in the laps of our sons and daughters? A lot. Back in 1989 a small book made a lot of sense: *50 Simple Things You Can Do to Save the Earth.* It sold 1.6 million copies and was followed by a sloo of books including *1001 Ways to Save the Planet* and *1001 Ways to Heal the Earth*

Some of those fifty ideas have become widespread and almost automatic like recycling and insulating homes. Some have found new popularity like compact fluorescent light bulbs which progressed to LEDs, and taking your own bag to the grocery store. Some have become laws like prohibiting unleaded gas, and mandating service stations to recycle motor oil. Some were popular slogans, like *save the rainforests*. And some caught on slowly, like car pooling, and then went uber fast into car sharing. Hey, aren't we all car pooling together in Grand Civil Supreme on its last fast rush towards the Bridge. Full speed and farewell, my Der.

Here are a few dramatic, silly, green actions that I have not seen covered elsewhere: Scream. When you go into Office Depot or Office Max, yell at them about the price of recycled paper. Then they can yell back at the tree chomping paper companies like Weyerhaeuser. Ask then if they know it uses less energy, less chemicals, and therefore less pollution in the air and water to re-cycle paper? And it's cheaper. So scream: "What the hell! If it costs less, why are you selling it for more?"

And if they repeat the propaganda from the lumber mills that it is cheaper to use new trees than to recycle, ask them about the government subsidies given by the US Forest system to cut down virgin, I cringe, yes violate and then kill virgin trees. Ask them if they subtract these subsidies and the cost of transporting the lumber to the mills (since you can bet they will calculate the cost of transporting the used paper to their mills). Only when the calculations most favorable to the lumber/paper mills are made, can they show that copier paper, only copier paper, is slightly cheaper to make from trees. Most other recycled papers are equal or and much cheaper to make.

But try to buy recycled paper for about the same price. When you can't, fill your lungs, open your mouth, and you know what to do.

I do to. I learned it from my sister, a professional, effective lawyer. She taught me that the best way to handle a merchandise dispute, if you thought you were being unfairly treated, was to RAISE YOUR VOICE. I tried it twice, and it worked both times. One of those times a large store manager looked hard at me and I knew he wanted to meet me in the back of the store, not right there where I was black balling his store in front of his customers.

I bought a ten ream box of paper made from pulp wood (I hope no pristine virgins were in there) for $30 because the recycled would have cost me $40. I felt bad. I was torn. I wanted to patronize the green product, but if I paid the high price, would that keep it high? (How's that for a great rationalization!) But if we all bought only recycled paper, then market forces would bring the price down. But if only a few bought recycled, the price would stay up there. I was not among the few good men. I can rationalize *ad infinitum*...

Ultimately paper kills the trees which clean our air and give us mouth-to-fresh-green-leaf-resuscitation. If that image doesn't give you leaf licking oral satisfaction, overlay the image of a tree's branches on the bronchial and alveoli of your lungs. Paper also gulps water--a pulp mill uses about 15 million gallons of water a day. For a while the e-storage looked like it would abolish paper, but making hard copies (paper) and faster printers, and lazy readers like me, actually increased paper usage. Magnetic storage seemed so frail. Now, though, cyber servers, the cloud, large external hard drives (and still the safer DVDs) save much in tiny spaces: a flash drive can hold all the 500 books of Isaac Asimov, the world's most prolific writer, on a chip smaller than my thumbnail.

Finally I back solely to electronic, plastic storage, and slowly I am re-using all my stored copies of all my wonderfully unread manuscripts. (But don't, absolutely don't recycle this book, even after the last uman on earth has read it and it is no longer a collectors' item). What to do with it? Keep it under your pillow, Der.

But do remember to scream at the price of recycled paper when you buy your office supplies. It embarrasses the store manager, angers the clerk, scares the customers, and makes an ass out of yourself. Scream anyway. The echo will resonate. I hate to soften my hyperboles, because you are smart enough to do so, but if you are laughing too hard, you may miss the application.

If screaming isn't your thing to help the world, maybe duct tape will do it—no, not on your mouth, but on your feet--I know one well-off friend who duct tapes his gym shoes. This same gentleman re-uses the waxed paper lining in cereal boxes to wrap sandwiches, and he is quite willing to pay extra to buy a Prius. That's dedication to the environment! Friend I salute you. You know who you are.

But if you are a stuck-up suburbanite like me, who would not be seen dead wrapped in duct tape, then instead of roses, at least use dandelions on your coffin. And here's how to pick them, not poison them: where I live, people look on dandelions as a yellow, neighborhood cancer. I would not have lived there, but the good schools weren't in the woods. So I kill dandelions to be a friendly neighbor who is not seeding their lawns. I admire dandelion's survival tactics: deep tap roots, their wind born seeds, and their sun-bold beauty. But at least I have quit carpet-bombing my lawn four times a year with fertilize/weed-kill. I reduced that to one time but the dandelions laughed. Then I got a squirt bottle and shot it into their smirking lion's teeth, one at a time. But just this morning (really not knowing I would write this, a neighbor who was having fun with his kids as "dandelion spotters," I got out the old metal forked tool, and pried them loose. No poisons! And they can still make a wine, grace a salad, or a coffin.

And if you don't want to save the flower for wine or passage to the next life, you can torque them out with your foot if you don't like to bend.

I am an earth hero at last! And screw what the dandelions might think.

To prove I am an earth hero, my son has started me buying used clothes. I wash them, then wear them like I always had them. Maybe humbling, but good for the earth.

We already know what to do about the energy issue—I've beat the H into you. If we used the big Hydrogen, it would prevent a lot of wars (and the unmentionable rising thermometer).

But let's not be a mono-fix-hated-anal-idiot!

Let's remember the Sun, Wind, and Waves.

Now I'll SHoWW you how you'll never forget those renewable, non-polluting life treasures. It's in the great acronym, SHoWW: Sun Hydrogen (forget the little o) Wind Waves. Showw. That's simple.

And if you want to get aggressive-in-your-face, add *up* to show: now you have *Showw Up* which could stand for nothing other than: U-Polluters! So when you are addressing a group of Neanderthals (to whom we smaller brained unmen have given a bad rap) just tell them to *show up*. They won't know they were insulted, and you can bet they have not read this far, though I hope they have laid their money down for the book. The title might deceive the violent and the NASCAR fans.

So we know the energy solution: *SHoWW*. Let's all push for it! We can have all the energy we want! This isn't like a diet. We can eat all the chocolate we want. Use all the good energy we wish, without getting fat. What's the matter with that? Not a damn thing. All those best things in life are free. The sun, the wind, the waves, the hydrogen in the water. Drink up! Breathe up! (Of course the minor caution—if you over-pig out on anything, you pay. Too much sex—sore. Too much sun—burned. Too much H—

smothered. Too much wind and waves—use your own imagination.

And for those microminded unmen looking for a hole in my argument, chocolate is an exception to the pig-out rule. But if you have to look for holes you are blind.

E is connected with M. That's the matter. We can get pure E fairly easily (try a sun burn) but to get photo voltaic cells takes some matter to make the cells. And metal is used in the structure of the tower and neodymium in the turbines to give us the "free" energy. So selecting our matter, matters, but is still doable and far better than the massive destructive "matters" used in coal and oil. Again Der, we are *aware*, we can think, we can decide, we can do.

Our thinking tells us to use renewable resources.

That's simple. Renewable.

Do we have to say that again before we start using it? Why won't we use only that matter that fits into the natural pattern of nature, and use it no faster than nature provides it, no faster than nature recycles it, and only if nature recycles it. Does this mean we do like the Old Dutch and make windmills out of wood? But, if the manufacturers also use clean energy to mine, transport, and manufacture, then the windmill will sing more happily, guiltless in the wind, and will not blink when a bird winks out of the sky. (If I have just *ouched* any ornithologists feelings, cats kill three thousand times the number of birds than windmills, and windows in buildings kill far more than the cats.

Then comes the job of re-cycling. Soda cans get crunched easier than aluminum windmills—but hey, we have some big feet. That is quite a pleasant podiatric problem, for it would mean we had installed enough windmills to facilitate a re-cycling system.

So for almost everything except your heart valve, which might be recycled from a pig, buy used, re-use, re-cycle.

And if you absolutely must buy new because you're finicky about buying Clinton's used underpants which he donated to charity a long time ago, then only buy those new items which can be naturally cycled with the earth and air and water.

That way, parts of those underpants won't come back to you in your food or air.

And search out those companies who manufacture with as much clean energy as possible and with as little harmful impact on our earth as possible. Check your Green Pages and let your fingers do the walking.

Damn it! Check your online phone book. My phone book has White pages that has you and me listed, Der; and it has Yellow pages for our giant commercial machines tucked neatly into the trunk of Grand Civil; and it has Red pages doubling up for those same people. Why not Green Pages? I love to be first with an idea, but after I wrote the above I discovered the *National Green Pages*, published by Co-op America. The Green Pages exist! And there are more than one set. They are helpful! Google them and support the green vendors..

Vote. Vote again. Call. Call again. Call local and Washington offices. E-mail. E-mail again, and again and again and again. You can actually vote 6 times: phone, letter, email to both local and Washington. It's easy! Just change a few words, and then do it again saying this is the second time you are writing, and ask when action will occur. Letters are time-consuming, but they are weighted the heaviest. Your order of communicative influence from top down goes: big donations, smaller donations, letters, phone calls, e-mails, and curses. (Unless of course you curse loudly and in the proper public place. See "The Scream" above, and adapt to "The Curse."

You can of course blog, flog, facebook, and tweet until they surrender. An ex prisoner was one of the most influential people to wake up Congress to the need to control the electronic voting machines.

And donate. Donate a little to each party's candidate and you'll buy access. And just to take the hypocrisy out of this, place the big bucks on the horse you believe in and promote him/her into the winner's circle.

I like to save money. I'm as tight as a sphincter about to...I used to go around the house to turn off lights to lower the bill. Now I turn them off to put less crap into the air from our enlightened, coal-burning power plants of Portland General Electric. I would even turn off lights at my college, where I didn't lower my bill, but I did raise the quality of our air.

My wife eats less food because she does not want to double waste/waist it. Both are real. Both good motivations for eating less, waisting less.

A gentleman named Steve Hagen (he said I could name him) came over and fixed my dryer. My wife and I hung out the wash for that day; I blush, for I could do that more often). Steve told me he cuts the tops out of frozen juice cans, and then recycles the metal and cardboard separately! Amazing refined recycling!

Let's all go neurotically small and then we will save megalomanically big! When I was a kid I would collect the insides of cigarette packs and gum wrappers and try to get a gigantic aluminum ball. I did so, often, and that ball would become large and densely pressed by loving little fingers and you would not want to be hit in the head with it. But the world would want to recycle it, for aluminum is valuable.

Hey! Let's put the kids onto this, like the kids of WWII who recycled cans and grease for military uses. If we did it to blow someone up, why not do it to save the world? I threw the idea out, now it is your job to start it in the schools. Like the paper drives. And the schools could make sure that it got actually recycled, and not tossed into a landfill by a lazy collection company which pretended to recycle.

Pushing the nanonuttyneurotic recycling, I separated the pieces inside the plastic bag that contained a printing cartridge, and recycled them. And I won't tell you the contrary stories of what I have seen average Americans casually toss away.

Waste Management, along with the Bank of America, have hyped their greenness in some ads. When the bankers and the garbage men go green, hey! Green is the happening color. Even if it is just green make-up, it will make the color go up in prestige. Garbage can do that for you.

On a spring day of April in 07, Home Depot labeled about 2,000 products with their Eco Options label. They probably heard our screams about recycled paper over at Office Max. Good pipes, Der. Home Depot tested the concept in Canada. It worked. They hope to add another 4,000 labels in the next two years. Although some of their interpretations of what is eco friendly are far fetched, let's buy Eco Options to make sure it works here.

A summary analogy struck me, and since I love analogies, I will strike you with it. I was choosing a spring green color from a computer palette for my website. I darkened it with some gray and the green turned ominously threatening. Let's reverse the process. Gradually let's see how much of the dark we can take out of ourselves, and how much of that natural spring green we can grow in ourselves.

We humans are as natural as we are unnatural, for we are actors and authors. In the words of Chardin, a visionary who sixty years ago wrote of the human phenomenon: "In the great game that is being played, we are the players as well as being the cards and the stakes …this… has hardly been formulated as yet in man's heart…"

Players. Cards. Stakes. Reflect on that. Power. Responsibility. And even now, that insight has barely formulated in our hearts.

Sure some environmental scientists are screaming, well, researching, analyzing, testing, concluding, and reporting— about that promise I made not to mention the temperature of the earth. But are their reports and Chardin's insight coming into our hearts? Our way of living?

In this great game of the cosmos, earth, nature, religion-- whatever you believe or think-- we are the players, we are active, we impact this great game of the earth; and we are the cards, so how we use us, and others, and our human resources is how we play the game.

And we are the stakes. The stakes don't get any higher than that, baby. Our asses are the chips in the game. We are betting our life.

Sure, we are not betting it all in one pot. But take a look at that pile of chips in front of you. Shrinking. (Forget those people who do want smaller derrieres). And what about your child sitting beside you, looking up at you and saying: "Daddy, Mommy, when I grow up to be like you, will there be any chips for me to play with?"

And where are you throwing your chips? Sure, some go right into that enormous intake pipe, hundreds of meters wide, that sucks down into the gas tank of the Grand Civil Supreme, which carries us all inside. And some of your chips are tossed into that trunk, which of course easily holds your house and other toys. But lest this image grow too bizarre, let's hold that image for a while. It took several generations to put everything into the trunk. If the house image doesn't work for you yet, just toss into it your other toys, all of which burn gas. They told me in classrooms, not to mix metaphors. But then, there was a lot they didn't tell me in classrooms, and a lot I didn't tell, and a lot I'm trying to make up for.

In poker terms, in our game of life, let's hope this book is part of the tell.

Let's hope we ante up, small at first in our life styles, then larger with renewable, clean energy for our homes and the H-Car, and in the interim, the electric car.

So what can we do?

Buy green.

In the much abused, little used, mantra: *buy used, use, re-use, recycle.*

Don't buy it if you can't recycle it. Don't do it, if it is harmful.

Now we can't instantly stop everything, but we can start stopping.

Here's a summary of the three biggies:

Houses.

If you are lucky enough to build new—build green. Energy efficient everything. Check it out. Google it. Do it. Currently the price of a green home is comparable with standard construction when you calculate the energy savings. And calculate the happiness and health.

Cars.

If you can afford one of the prototypes, hydrogen, drive all you want. You are in hydrogen heaven, and I will worship you as a saint. If you can get a natural gas supply, awesome. A hybrid, you are doing great, better than most of us. A small, high mph car, you're trying, and risking a little against those SUV suckers. Bike? Walk? You're a hell of a lot healthier and happier than fat car potatoes like I. Just smile when I buzz by you in my insult mobile--instead of flicking off the car crazies like I do.

Things.

I'm not going to get intimate and tell you what lingerie to buy, but apply the same principles to appliances, furniture, clothing, and food (buy local if you can from farmers who are organic and respect the land—again, you will be healthier). I haven't broken anything on the parking lot pavement since I started carrying out goods without bags, and the larger loads in cloth bags, again and again.

Money.

Put your money where your heart is—green. Invest your money, including your pension, where you can control it. One of my kids castigated me for considering buying oil stocks. I knew they would go up. But that was wrong in his morality, and he was right. He'll just have a smaller inheritance, but he is happier and you can breathe just a molecule fresher.

Take your kids and grandkids into what woods are left. Sixty years ago Rachel Carson asked that we give our children a sense of wonder, and told us that "the more clearly we can focus our attention on the wonders and realities of the universe about us, the less taste we shall have for destruction."

It's up to you, Generation H! A challenge to Xers, Yers, Millennials, Zers...to metamorphosize into Generation H. Don't be the unmen. Place the big H in front, and become the new superhero, the Human! The Hydrogen Generation! Generation H! There, now you have a lot of names, hopefully not an identity complex, but hopefully a clear definition of a profound purpose in life. I would be proud to be called any of those.

And citizens, even you old fogies, bleached and wrinkled from the Great White Out, you silent generation, wake up; you baby boomers, grow up; let's all prod Congress. Let's get together, form groups, and let Congress know what we want, and that we are watching their votes, and that our vote is pending.

So my Der green traveler in Civil with me at this moment of time, we have arrived at this place in time unthinkingly. Now let's stop this insanity of our massive cultural inertia. Let's pull hard on the wheel of the Car of State. It is massive. It is speeding. Some say too fast, and too impossible to change directions. Let us brake. Let us disembark. Alive. And steer a new Car of State into a new world, taking us to a clean green tech in which we can live. What else are we to do? Or as Tolstoy asked: "How then do we live?" We have only begun to answer that question as we have become aware. Remember that omitted *"a"* in Der? Dear Environmentally Aware Reader, since we are aware, then we can think, then we can know, then we can do.

And what more can we do?

We can begin to listen to our children.

We can begin to help them deal with the problems we are passing on to them.

We can help them with our networks.

We can loosen up some of our money before we die.

We can give them our moral support.

We can give them, most importantly, our love.

Meanwhile, until they reach energy utopia, we need to start the process. We need to keep squeezing that dirty energy down until it approaches zero.

the green hope

The giant car hums smoothly,
Drumming the passengers into oblivion.

Bridge Out!

Twenty, thirty, forty yards or years away.
    stone, steel, death gapes.
The drowsy passengers cruise cushy
    towards the smashing death of
civilization.
Father partially forgive the drivers,
    semi-conscious of what they do.
Father don't forgive us,
    if we don't find out what we do.
And Father, damn us all if we still stomp on
    the gas.

    My Dad helped create our mechanical world, I
retreated into the Great White Out, but my children are
green and growing. Once again, Der, forgive me if I do not
credit your children enough, but mine are those whom I

know best, and besides, I get to brag because my fingers are on the keyboard.

We were young once, Der, dancing flowers in the 60s and floating dreams up into a world that could only glow brighter. Remember how our parents proudly said: "Step inside, enjoy the ride." And we mounted Civil Supreme.

Do you think they would have placed us there if they knew the danger?

When our children were born, just as proudly we sat them in Civil. Sure, we knew a bit more of the boom crash instant death, so we added seat belts, baby seats, and air bags, but we knew little of the lethal, larger danger leaking unseen out the back of our car. So our kids grew up like us, and young, they did what we did. And they danced and drove guiltlessly.

Shake us wake us! We dreamed. We lived that dream and thought it was true love, until Love Canal became a Hooker, nuclear wastes piled up in rusting barrels, mountain tops blown away, rainforests chewed up-- the flowers began to wither, species vanished, and the world choked and coughed. Gleaming tech dulled, tarnished, and spewed invisible poisons into our air and waters.

May our sons and daughters forgive us, for we have given them an injured earth. But we awoke, half groggily, in the Great White Out.

It is to my children that I owe my awakening.

I am lucky, or troubled, to have four kids who have honked the horn, hit the brakes, and shown me the looming gulf ahead. They are far more aware than I of their addiction to Civil.

I see it now. Driving has become a habit I like, and almost need as a condition of living in a suburb (blush) and driving to work. I used to call myself "educated but educable." Now I call myself "miseducated but hopefully still educable." Therefore, I can try. I can try to turn. Help me Der. It ain't going to be easy. The steering wheel is huge and it has so many many hands, big hands, mechanical hands with giant corporate fingers gripping the wheel, holding it firmly against us. Those large hands lust upon the feel of the wheel and the hum of the road. Their heads are smart. They can read the sign. But they see the road as rich for them, and they don't care about their children in the car.

Ride the rich road while you can, and to hell with the rest of the world.

And it is the rest of the world.

For the drivers of huge Civil have not just splattered a few birds off their windshields, or smashed a squirrel or two, or even collided with a deer—they have ridden over and squashed to death uncounted species making us, umen, the extinguishers of life forms. And that was in our recent the past. And now ahead--bridge out, full speed.

Much of the rest of the living world rides with us, pesticidal, zoicidial, homicidal, globicidal unmen.

Wake up world. And you, Gary, wake up yourself!

As I listen to my children trying to wake me from this insidiously narcotizing dream, I would like to make an author comment. This book continues to be biographical, but I am going to blend my children and not use their names. They are of age, and I have no right to speak for them. But they damn well better read this book and listen to their father's advice which, after all, is much of their own. And most of the time I'll just refer to them as my kids, just cause it's shorter than children.

I almost called this section *The Green Generation* when I googled it almost a decade ago. Only 457 hits, but that was so low that I was tempted to claim ownership but I must maintain my masquerade of honesty. Can I at least claim independent creativity? Anyhow, I probably heard the term subconsciously somewhere before—maybe from my wife. Often when I exclaim my great ideas out loud, my wife looks at me hopelessly and says: "Hon, I just said that five minutes ago."

I've got it! When I told my kid about the new name for his generation, he didn't tell me to shove off (who wants their old man naming their group—hey, I named you kid). Instead he said that he was not sure how green his generation was. He got me thinking, and a new name came:

The Greening Generation!

That's it! It is more accurate because it has a progressive sense, it has a nice double meaning of greening the earth and becoming green themselves, and it passed the google test for originality—only two hits! And one of them on a website that lasted only two months and did not actually name the generation, and the other on a Girls Gone Wild Video—I didn't check into it very far, but I imagine it's just some coeds painting their breasts green. Nothing wrong with that, since our Anglo-Saxon ancestors used to paint their bodies blue, and fight naked. These greenies would probably just make love. And if you don't have Anglo-Saxon blood, you can choose either blue or green for whatever part you wish to pain.

The Greening Generation! A second candidate to add to the H Generation. You read it here first, now go and become it and help those with the age credentials to become it. And if you have a snotty, littering, polluting, anti-earth little kid, make him help you paint the house green and accidentally spill the paint on him. At least he'll look green. You also read that parenting technique here, for the first time, and I don't even have to google that one to check it out. It will work. I know. A respected psychologist told me that when his mother slapped him in the face with a fish because he was a lippy kid and said: "I've always wanted to do that," he had an awakening moment. Green paint dumped accidentally on your kid could be that awakening moment.

One of my greening kids said something that totally destroyed my cushy life: "Dad, I challenge you to show me one thing in this room that hasn't hurt our earth." This book is strongly indebted to that comment and that kid. And this book, too, has hurt the earth—but I have made it available in e-form for 99¢ to lessen the impact. (Please don't think my writing is that worthless--I really value my words disproportionately high; and in the 1980s an organization sold my writing for a buck a word! Now, if you wish to compensate me appropriately, start counting the words).

But back to my greening kid who disrupted my cozy life--I was sitting in the den and I looked around at the TV, couch, and magazines to quickly meet and refute his challenge. Nothing! There was nothing in that room that hadn't hurt the earth in its making or in its transporting. In fact, in my whole house there was nothing! Not even the potted plants. Think about the pot the plant is in. How the plant was raised, fertilized. How the plant got transported through the garden center into my home.

Hey—quit nosing in my environmentally destructive home, and check out your own. I pass my son's challenge to you to find anything in your home that hasn't hurt the earth. Think a second before you keep reading. Okay, smart Der, so you picked up a rock on one of your nature strolls, and you didn't even have to drive the rock home, but you walked. Unless you were naked and used no shoe material, and unless you ate organic food for the energy to carry that rock, you hurt the earth.

Am I going too far? (I hope so—I never wanted to stop when the girls said "no.") I know you want to throw that stone at me. Go ahead, you with the stone and without sin, cast the first stone. Hey, I want to stone myself. I feel sick in this sick culture. This is the total, awful cultural bind we find ourselves in. The giant doors of Civil are slammed shut. And we are moving deadly fast.

Stunningly, all four of my kids are of the greening generation, working for our earth. The oldest studies the land from the Rockies to the Himalayas as a geologist. One straddles the creeks and kayaks the rivers as an ichthyologist; he calls himself the Riverwalker. One takes blood, bone, muscle and hair samples from bears and then does impressive lab work, and the last works for an NGO trying to conserve the land. That one, and possibly all of them, could probably write much better books than this one.

I'd like to claim the credit for these kids, but I can't, unless they are reacting to an energy intoxicated dad. I give their mother credit, and I got lucky. They tell me that they are greener than their greying Dad (not the shades of fifty, cause I'm older but just as bad), but because I took them camping.

Being a teacher, we took our two older sons on long summer weeks camping in the western mountains. We paused for a while with our next two children, but when we asked our two oldest what they liked best about our parenting, so we could get it right the second time, the answers were: "Get a dog," and "Take them camping." We did both, and the dogs barked and the mountains sang to them, and they heard the songs in their blood, and began their quests.

Since I am an English teacher, how did the woods root in me? Again, I got lucky as a child to have always had some small woods tucked nearby my homes. I'd like to attribute that to my parents, but a large part of it is probably due to the glaciers that left Cincinnati hillier than Rome. Those little woods saved me, connected me to the disappearing earth. Half consciously as a parent, I then looked for a little green to surround our homes, and maybe that, as well as the camping, helped connect our kids to the earth.

Note to my wife in case she reads this far: when I am speaking of my children and saying "I," almost always I should include you since most of our children's goodness comes from you. But since you dislike my vulgar vocabulary, and still have not read some of my nasty books, I will use "I" and take all the credit because you might never read this to know that I have stolen your goodness, your brightness, your beauty, and your love—and I and my children are life-long grateful. I was going to say "eternally grateful," but I can't promise myself an afterlife. At least not a quality one.

And maybe we can't promise too many more generations that they will have life on earth. Not if we don't get going. Getting going is partially the theme of this section—you know, pass the buck to the greening kids, since they are going to get all the bucks anyhow, those that their colleges haven't gotten already.

And joining nature with college, here's how one of my kids explained it all in an application letter to a college:

Beauty, grandeur, stature, wilderness, solitude, wildlife: what's in a mountain? Of all the places I have been, nothing can ever compare to the mountains. Every summer I return to Wyoming, Montana, Colorado, Washington, or Oregon. The mountains of these states I consider a second home and hope to reside there permanently some day.

The annual trip West began some eight years ago when my brother was attending graduate school in Albuquerque. My family visited him and instantly I was enthralled by the intricate labyrinth of canyons, deserts, and mountains. The next year we braved Wyoming where we camped for two weeks among the Rockies. Then arose the mountain of my mind, the one that is always there—massive, snow-domed Mount Rainier.

There is something incomprehensible and awe-inspiring about a towering granite mountain, so sure of its invincibility as to seem almost arrogant. Or perhaps it's simply the stark contrast between the suburban life, always one step away from a grimy, crowded city, to the unadulterated peacefulness of utter wilderness. There is something blissful in escaping mankind's technology and vacationing with nature. It makes me feel alive, and, for once, realize that I am a part of the whole, part of the planet Earth. We are simply residing in an intricate and beautiful network of ecosystems, a network of many layers of life, and we are not separate from it. Mountains are the eternal opiate of the human race, always ready to give an exhilarating rush, at once both life-affirming and humbling.

I didn't ask my son for permission to quote him, so he could sue me for being the intellectual property thief that I am. Yep. I've just used my kid for this chapter as I used my Dad to develop the Silver Shadow, to develop our theme of our growing awareness of the idiocy of what we are doing. And worse, instead of bearing a parent's burden, I'm laying the really heavy stuff on them—the challenge to undo our damage and begin the healing. To help them in this small task, they are all equally in my will--they are welcome to the leftovers of my hefty teacher's pension.

So kids, I won't embarrass you anymore than I always do, and I just want you to know that you can use me as I have used my Pop--and I loved him, and I love you. I also love the mountains, oceans, rivers, trees, plants, animals (I'm omitting insects, because of the mosquito—that makes me a speciesist—like a racist) and humans, yes I love humans. It may not seem so since I have ripped at our life style, but I do. Have I told you lately, Der, that I love you, too?

Maybe my kids will meet your kids, Der, and form a small group. And hopefully that massively empowering dictum from Margaret Mead will unfold. We have quoted it before, but let it ring again!

Never doubt that a group of thoughtful, committed citizens can change the world. Indeed, that is all that ever has.

But our children too, caught in the world we created, drive to survive. If the traffic hurtles at high speed, if the river rages, isn't it better to go with the flow, to swim with the current? No, I take that back. I don't want to offer a slogan to Exxon to allow them to suck us deeper into the evil of oil. (Obviously oil isn't evil of itself. Dead dinosaurs are not the blame. It's the users. I was just enamored of the phrase, so I'll say it again.) *The evil of oil.* So there, Exxon, go slime yourself. Have a drink on me. I'll buy you a whole barrel, even at your prices, if you'll drink it.

Yes, to survive the flood we must swim with the current momentarily, but we can start cutting diagonally downstream across the current! It's easy. Use your hands as rudders, as I found out so sputteringly in the Mississippi. We can make it to shore. We can drag our soiled bodies out, we can look at the current and see if that is the way to live, to swim with it, with all the chemicals pouring towards yet another Gulfendofitall, which is really the same foreboding gulf beyond the Bridge Out sign.

Or is there a better way to cleaner waters? Far-sighted environmentalists and water sucking capitalists (and the thirsty) see water as more important than oil (after all you can live only 5 or 6 days without water. You can live forever—till you die—without oil. And in fact, you will live longer without oil).

All of my children have, at times, worked with our waters of life. One kid has analyzed the geomorphic impact of the great rivers of China. He has sampled the millions of metric tons of silt pouring into the Yangtze river from the Tibetan Plateau towards the Three Gorges Dam as China emulates our damn mistakes. And from the Kunlun mountains, surprising close to the headwaters of the Yangtze, springs the Huang He, (Yellow River) which for six months of the year barely makes it to the sea. Quite similar to our Colorado River, where you can go to its mouth and kiss a pair of dry lips. Lately, though, we have started de-salinating and letting a little more water into Mexico, so maybe you can get a wet kiss.

And I repeat, don't knock China which pollutes about one-fourth as much per person as us, even while making most of our goods. Even though China has a company worth over a trillion dollars, China National Petroleum Corp's market capitalization is larger than Exxon and GE combined, and even though China is aggressively seeking and buying oil all over the world, China is also growing its alternate energies faster than the U.S, so much so that Americans are investing in China's energy companies, like Cleantech China was a hot stock as far back as ten years ago. You go, China!

Rivers (when they get there) flow into lakes and seas. Let's get Russia into the big G-20 polluting industrial nations. Russia has the largest fresh water lake in the world (the five great lakes together are larger, and I'm not counting the Caspian Sea—hey, come on—it has the name "Sea" and it is pretty salty). Russia has spewed and sucked this largest lake, Lake Baikal, into a shallow saline mess less than a fourth its former size. Let's not knock Russia's treatment of its lakes—Texas has only one natural lake, Caddo Lake, which is currently being overgrown with silvania molesta—sounds nasty. But what is Texas doing to prevent the growth of this plant? Spraying it with herbicide. Herbicide into their one natural lake? We can pretty much figure that the suffix *cide,* with its parallel with homi*cide,* is not a particularly nice thing to spray into your drinking water.

California might go one better. It is currently considering dumping 17,000 pounds of fishicide (that's one *cide* up the staircase of death from herbicide, one *cide* closer to you and me) into Lake Davis to kill the Northern Pike. They love that fish up there in Wisconsin. And we used to love you Californians.

If we suck rivers dry, and poison lakes, can un-men be far behind?

Back to the other river rats, I mean kids. One studied biodiversity in the Amazon tributary system along the Tiputini River, and dipped samples from the Milwaukee rivers to run bacteria counts for the Great Lakes Water Institute.

A third kid is a Friend of the River and worked on the Milwaukee River. He was the one who showed me the mud and the muck in which I was smothering. Unfortunately when I fed back to him some dirty data about his Cannon River in Minnesota, he still swam in it. When will they ever learn? And who was the Mississippi swimming father who modeled for him.

Did we ever learn? And it is to these kids who won't learn from our mistakes, that we are handing our graying world to, trusting them to green it? Fortunately this son is smart enough, like my wife, to not read my books, so he will not find this slam. He will miss one high point of praise, though, so there, you unreader!

But one son who will be reading this is the river king. He is called The Riverwalker. He monitors the streams and rivers of Northwestern Oregon that flow from the Coastal Mountains into the Pacific Ocean. He tracks the salmon and steelhead trout rushing into the many streams, checking to see if they can mount the ladders, analyzing the health of the banks of the waters, watching which fish spawn and die, noting the number and location of the reeds where the eggs are deposited, and seeing the fry and fingerlings gather in the pools until they are big enough to face the sea. We thank you Riverwalker, and the unknown others like you who wish and want and will keep our waters clean. As an unavoidable aside because of parental privilege, in the summer of 07 The Riverwalker married the Land Steward of an NGO. River and Land met! A merger impossibly beautiful!

One of the kids recommended that I read *Beyond the 100th Meridian.* How close we came to settling our country in a water conscious way! But we missed. To see the disastrous results, read *The Cadillac Desert.*

John Wesley Powell (1834-1902) the hero of *Beyond the 100th Meridian,* was the American Proteus. He rowed the entire Ohio twice, did the Wisconsin, Illinois, and Missouri rivers, and stunningly, the Colorado twice in a wooden boat! And with only one arm. He wanted the West to be settled not along congressional townships which cut the earth like it a pan of brownies into artificial right angles of baselines and meridians and ranges. Rather, profoundly and brilliantly and naturally, he wanted people to live where the water was, to settle where the land was naturally fertile. Such uncommon sense! Powell came within one vote in Congress of settling land according to Nature's waters. Mother knew best. One of her prescient children, John, listened to her.

If we had followed this principle of living near water, LA would be a small city of about 9 thousand people, and it wouldn't have to fight water wars and steal rivers from farmers and orchards, and strive to negotiate water deals with Oregon, Washington, and even Canada. Do you see many rivers in LA? A lot of freeways, but not water. Underneath all that concrete, LA is still a desert with the gaping mouth of a thirsty giant sucking for all the water it can get.

There's a green wind a-blowing, and it's been there a while but we are only beginning to hoist our sails. Let's not pass this free, exhilarating source of energy off to future development, as the oil and most energy companies would like.

Let's hear it for the wind! There's a green wind a-blowing! Someone write a song.

In 1888, Charles Brush built the first electric generating windmill that sent 12 kilowatts into his home at 37th and Euclid Avenue in Cleveland, Ohio. Thomas Edison built his own wind powered home and he wanted to build a larger one to supply groups of homes. And now windmill farms are growing! In 2014 Denmark let the wind blow 39.1% of their free, breathable energy right into their generators. They hope to soon allow the wind to blow 50%. In 2004 my son's college, Carleton, dedicated a windmill that gave them about 30% of their energy. In 2011 they added a second and reached 50%. We passed up Denmark! Ooops. That was just on a single campus, not nationwide. A rivaling nearby college saw the result and put up. Now that's a little fresh air.

Expect attacks. Expect attacks from the air defilers. And even expect them to twist your sympathies and use them against you. Deviously, those energy trolls use the airy spirits of color and song, our birds, to attack windmills. They say windmills kill birds.

I've briefly mentioned this but let's get some stats (okay, the numbers are a little old): A government report from the National Research studied bird deaths in 2003, and estimated that 37 thousand birds died from wind turbines. Okay, that seems like a lot of birds, but let's put that into perspective and watch the real killers: cats. Hundreds of millions of birds per year. But cats are small compared to our houses, buildings, and power lines which smashed and fried over a billion! (SFC 5/4/07). And how many birds die from the air pollution, toxic water, and poisoned insects?

Sorry birds. The few who die from windmills, die now just from us, but for your own cause: those dead will be honored by a flyover in formation from the many birds who now fly in the purer air that the windmills save from the coal and oil villains. The air was yours in the first place, so sorry we fouled it up (no pun, I just saw it while editing, if you believe I edit). The windmills are actually one of our best hopes so you can fly free, and we both breathe freely.

So, how dangerous are windmills? If I have pushed the right calculator buttons, windmills account for only .00003 of one percent of bird killings. My front window rivals that amount.

Once I stood beneath a flock of birds almost too thick to see through. Another equally thick and numerous flock was flying fast and directly into the other flock. I cringed awaiting the many collisions. I expected dead and wounded birds to begin dropping from the sky. There was not a single death.

Not a single feather.

Now I ask you, with that incredible agility and ability to dodge darting, moving targets, do you think a bird would have any trouble missing those huge blades of a wind turbine that do not change directions? I don't mean to slam birds here, but if a bird didn't dodge them, then it was old and time to die, or it had a Quixote complex.

If you were a bird and had the choice of flying over a smokestack from a Wisconsin coal-burning power plant or through a windmill, what would you choose? The one would be deadly, the other fun, flirting with the big, slow, dumb wings of the wind turbine, like a small bird chasing a hawk. That partially explains why so few birds die, and why windmills are actually bird friendly. (And don't cry about the few night birds who don't see and are drawn to the sound. You can cry only after you brick up your windows and stop killing birds. Better, promote windmills and save a lot of birds.)

So what time is it in this green and coming world? It's H-Time! Not the H-Bomb, which is a fitting reality and symbol for our nasty destructive nature—polluting, unknowing, and caring little unless we can see it in the form of dogshit or a bag of garbage tossed on our front lawn. Can't we open our provincial eyes and look at the larger polluting of the earth? That's it! A pair of goggles that lets us see the invisible mercury and arsenic and the hundreds of other poisons in our air that we put there. Now Google Glass, that's a better goggle to make!

So what time is it?

It's H-Time! H time bean, as I startled you with that piece of information, in 1807 when we had the first internal combustion car, and it was a Hydrogen Car. It's time now, high time for hydrogen. Time for the H-Train, the H-Plane, the H-Home—what the hell, it's time for the H-Age, the H-Era. What time is it? It's H-Time!

If you think I'm beating the H out of this concept and limiting it too narrowly or expanding it too universally, remember, H is the first element, H is the most common element in the universe (over 70%, but don't ask me who went out there and counted it), and H is 10% of you

And to get hydrogen, all we need is water, and then use the clean energy power of the sun and the wind to separate H_2O into oxygen and hydrogen.

The sun and the wind can give us pure Hydrogen!

So what time is it? It's H-Time! Hydrogenium! Hydrogéne! Wasserstoft! Idrogeno! Hidrogênio! Hidrógeno! Väte! Vodik! An H by any other name burns as sweet! But what's with this Väte and Vodik! Can't the Swiss and the Czechs spell? Who cares? I care, damn it. Don't those idiosyncratic narcissistic illiterate countries know that Cavendish discovered H, and he named it after the Greek for *Hydro* (water) and *Gennan* (generate)? And don't give me that rose by any other name crap, which I use only when it advances my own themes, such as poking fun at the Swiss--actually they have one of the strictest mph laws; they are the good guys environmentally even if somewhat shady economically. I didn't know all that etymological stuff either, but write, write now to the Czech Republic and Switzerland and demand that they quit using Väte and Vodik, and thus quit abusing the name of our first, our purest, our savior element. Otherwise, we will invite them over for the ride of their life on Civil and we will translate the English of *Bridge Out* as: *Have a Nice Day*! But be sure to praise them for their environmental policies.

Water generating! Cool name, that hydrogen. Much better than those hydrocarbons that can cause coughing and lung disease, or those nitrogen oxides that form ozone and acid rain, or that carbon monoxide that can distort your vision, cloud your thinking, and if you close the garage door can save you from the giant gulfendallofit; or that CO_2 that leads to that unmentionable hot earth. (I still did not mention it.) Water generating! Yes, much better than wheezing and rubbing red eyes and muddling minds and checking out of life's hotel at 4 in the morning.

And H does not stand for Hybrid cars. Even though we praise Toyota for having sold millions of hybrids worldwide. (They estimate they have avoided putting many billions of pounds of CO_2 in the air.) H does stand for Hydrogen cars such as BMW's Hydrogen 7, and Honda's FCX. In 2015 we are now seeing a choice of FCV, fuel cell vehicles that run on hydrogen gas and emit no harmful products. Check out Toyota and Honda.

Do not check out Elon Musk. What did I just say? I love Elon. But listen to the man who protests too much: he makes batteries to store electricity, and thus is in competition with Hydrogen. I think he's wrong on this one.

What time is it? No, it is not time to put this book down and go to bed because you have a H-eadache. I'm sorry. When I just called H our savior element, I do think I have found my god. If you are a tithing kind of person, send ten percent to me (I guarantee a better use than your average TV evangelist) and I'll send you a membership card. Actually, if you do send, I'll buy copies of this book and give them away free. Please do not interpret this as subtle begging. It's a blatant demand! Join the H-Church or join the Swiss and Czechs.

H-Time! Can we let it stand for pure, non-polluting energy, hydrogen as well as sun and wind. After all, the sun is a hydrogen fusion furnace and its heat partially drives our wind. So it is H-Time! Remember François Rivaz and the first Hydrogen car in 1807. Don't forget.

And how much time do we have left? While the green revolution is growing, the Great Grand Civil, invisible like a ghost, carries us all onward, increasing speed with a deadly intention. We have taken some of the stink from the diesels, but do we have to smell it before we know it? Sarin and carbon monoxide are odorless and deadly. Do we have to hurtle over the cliff before we see the gulf? Do we have to dive into the gulf before we see smashing death rushing up at us?

How long do we have left before the crash? I guessed a century and a half. "No Dad, not even that," came the response from one of my green kids.

Green groups are growing. Even groups that might at times appear anti-science. Witness The Evangelical Greens! They might have been instantly created, and frozen in time, but they are evolving as stewards of the earth! Another group, the Green Corps recruits students who will be activist environmentalists. My kid attended and met young green idealists from all over the country. He was encouraged, for he had thought his college was an isolated bit of sanity floating on a sea of insanity. Now he knows that there are other islands, other people, and if they could join hands, they could form a continent; and the continent could join Europe and Asia, and Africa and South America (oh yes, and that big island at the end of the archipelago) and all could once again become *Pangaea--all earth.* Maybe, one day, once again the earth will be whole. But only if unmen grow whole. If we don't, the earth, aided by us, will slap our species out of existence as we go down with those we have killed in the sixth mass extinction.

Nothing wrong with shops, but a lot wrong with Pandora. Back into your box girl. Humans need to retrofit her shops so they grow naturally from the earth. Civil Supreme can run on non-polluting hydrogen gotten from non polluting sources. I'll breathe to that!

But I'm ahead of myself, for this one's for my children.

Green is bursting out all over! Green Festivals in Seattle, Chicago, and even Washington D.C. Green is hot! I returned from the Green Festival in Chicago with hope in my heart from the 30,000 warm-spirited crowd, even as my head sagged knowing that that number was only about one-third of one percent of Chicago. But hey, we wouldn't have gotten our fingers on those creative, mouth bursting organic snacks at the festival. That'll increase next year's crowd.

Stunningly brilliant emeralds glowed everywhere, but one hero stood out. Dave Deppner who saw what the ravaged forests did to the people of the Philippines. He began planting their trees back in the 60s. One tree was the Ipil Tree, so this Johnny Ipil-Seed and his organization, Trees for the Future, continued through four decades to plant over 52 million trees. That's right. His cost has been about 10 cents a tree, and he has been at it with hundreds of volunteers over forty years.

From 1999 through about 2006 the Sanctuary-ABN-AMRO Wildlife gave awards to Earth Heroes who fought to protect the environment. Chander Singh Negi won the award in 2005 for fighting to protect the tiger. Ironic, isn't it, that this dominant animal needs "puny" umen protection?

If the tiger needs protecting, then what of the butterfly? What of the whole world? Stocks in renewable energy are finally climbing with solar and wind use. If they have dropped when you read this, rest assured they will climb for the next 50 years. Co-op America has a huge list of socially responsible green companies. Invest now! Help the green to go up, and the grey and the black to plunge.

Money.

I've been too positive in this Green Hope section, so here's a little sarcasm to cut the sanguine green.

CSO.

Can you guess it? You've heard of CEO, and CFO, and COO, and maybe CMO, CIO, and CTO (marketing, information, and technical), and believe it or not, a CLO—yes, a few companies have the euphemism of a chief learning officer—would that more of them did--but now, a CSO!

A Chief Sustainability Officer!

I should be ecstatic, but how can we not suspect that this is all pomp with no bucks? Less than 30% of them report to the CEO, so that determines their power. And what if you ask the company if they have a CSO and they say sure, while meaning a Sales, or a Security Officer? With cyber crime I am sure that those two will report directly to the CEO.

There is gilt or there is gold, green or fake pateen. *Pateen* is poetic for *patina*; and for those puritanical school marms who do not accept that rhyme, then take this: There is green and there is gold; there is gilt and there is mold.

So take your pick of the pateen or the mold, and be judged by your choice. Should we cheer or jeer for the CSO? Even if it is gilty, moldy, pateen? Hopefully the title of CSO is a nod to the public's growing awareness, a nod to what will become. If we help it.

The first two companies I found to have a CSO were Dow and DuPont. Actually I know nothing about how green art thou Dow, but Dupont, you are flickered with faint spots of pale pale green. Earlier, in 1944 the initials for Dupont were DDT, and then remember the Chlorofluorocarbons? They were better known as the freon in your refrigerator. Well, Dupont let those little monsters loose to gobble up the ozone which opened that hole above Antarctica. Dupont had to replace the CFCs, but heuristically, they made even more money. That started them green thinking—good thing, or we might have fried all those happy marching feet down there.

Dupont still has some major problems releasing carcinogens and hazardous chemicals, and they have slid one sleeper into your kitchen—don't go to sleep while you're cooking! Teflon can release poison gas in your kitchen if it gets too hot—some testing shows the poison is released at temperatures as low as 325° Fahrenheit, while DuPont says 660°. I almost lost a friend because I attacked Teflon as bad, and she refused to give up her Teflon. Was that a Teflon-coated friendship? Worse, I almost lost two children in a skillet that got white hot, way above the poison spewing temperature. I threw out all my skillets coated with Teflon, then I confess, I purchased one for stir fries. See how Pandora has her hooked nails under my skin? So far DuPont has settled some lawsuits in the multi-millions, and a multi-billion case is pending.

So, what to do? Return to that cast iron skillet, which can clock a burglar or a drunk husband much more effectively. No--buy ceramic.

But the pale green good news is that DuPont's release of carcinogens from 1990 to 2006 has declined 92%, and their hazardous waste has decreased from 2.2 billion (some measure or other) to 931 million (some measure or other—*Fortune* 4/07). That's why I colored them pale green.

Is 931 million of hazardous waste a positive pale color? Or still a sickly green? Anyhow, encourage DuPont; for whether motivated by money in sales, or money lost in lawsuits, or the damage they have done to you and me while smoothing the legs of ladies in nylons, they are making some changes.

A full page green-colored ad in the NYT stated that if all Americans who are buying dishwashers this year bought an Energy Star dishwasher from Bosch, it would save 3.4 million acres of forest. I haven't checked the calculations, but just the mere fact that the ad used green to appeal is great!

Money is green, and when green becomes the color of money, many more very wealthy people get interested. So—as a consumer, if we buy green, guess what happens?

Late in 2007 the New York Times ran a special business section entitled, "The Business of Green." One of the highlighted phrases: "The market tells producers: it's go green or goodbye." A lot of the greys have not yet gone goodbye, but they are fighting and yelling and starting to shrink slightly. Just relish that climactic phrase: go green or goodbye.

So all you closet greens, you can now come out, unwrap, and speak green, brag green, curse the earth destroyers, yell NIMBY! Not in My Biosphere Yahoo! More and more will grow green.

One fellow who did not sign up for a green organization I tried to get going said to me sheepishly, "I have two SUVs."

Sheepish is good, because it will be harder for that gentleman to buy the next SUV, and if more sheep grow green wool, and blah baa sheep do not follow the flock, there will be less polyester clothing--a small symbol of a huge looming cultural change. If we change it.

A stunning year for the sun! Utility scale generation increased almost 100% in 2014 compared to the same time in 2013 according to the U.S. Energy Information Administration. That is stunning! But stunningly sad, our total solar production is about 1% of our nation's energy usage. That is heavy, gloomy overcast: since the sun is almost the entire ultimate source of all of our energy, what is this paltry1%? Still, that industrial doubling is great, and let's continue to heat up the sun, which is already burning by itself, and doing just fine thank you.

Eight years ago, Clean Wisconsin forced a court review of Wisconsin Energy, which wished to dump 1.8 billion gallons of hot water each day directly into Lake Michigan instead of using cooling towers. Also they had a pipe ready to dump mercury-contaminated water into the Lake (*The Defender*, 2007).

Mercury! The madness. Drink up. Avoid Alzheimer's--kill your brain early. Fish love it too, so eat formerly heart-healthy, now mercury-fatted fish.

The Clean Wisconsin members are real heroes. It is easy for me to rant on these pages. It is hard to maintain the long clean fight in court. Thank you Clean Wisconsin!

Green mayors, mayors of the Green Party, have won elections in the smaller cities, the largest being Richmond, CA.

The party itself is the fifth largest in the country, with about a quarter million registered members, and it would have easily been a strong third if not for Ralph Nader. Nader was a hero when he was young for his consumer fights against GM and corporate America. He burned his hero mask when he took down Gore (and our country) in Florida, and even lying about how the Democratic party was not much better than the Republicans. The Green Party appealed to me before 2000. Damn you Ralph Vader.

I didn't start my kids off right. But they will change the world, starting with the small things like plastic. If the coastal countries dump 8 million metric tons of plastic a year into the ocean, how much do we make? It is more than steel now. Frightening. And you all know of those dozen or so plastic gyres, one 600 miles across. Take a canoe.

Do you recall that sexy ad of a woman in black lingerie holding a chain saw? Anyone with a castration complex, don't get excited. She symbolized Victoria's dirty secret of using hardwood trees to make their two million or so catalogs. I met Shanna Ortman of Forest Ethics who was working on the campaign pressuring companies to use paper made from fast growth pulp trees. Forest Ethics was successful and now I would like to re-announce that Victoria's catalog, as well as their lingerie, is clean! And sexy! Lust away with clean green dreams that are environmentally friendly. Thank you Forest Ethics!

Those with scatological sensitivities, skip to the next naughty item. I have already embarrassed you by stating you probably have six or more pesticides in your pee. But where do we put that pee. Should we drop five golden ounces and then flush with five gallons? Is there something wrong with that ratio? One of my kids came back from college with: *if it's yellow, let it mellow; brown flush it down.* That would save a lot of water. Actually pee might be great for the grass—lots of nitrogen. In Tawny Alley (my wonderful, departed golden retriever was named Tawny, and I'm surprised I am just now mentioning her, since she was of a higher order on the evolutionary line) the grass grew green. So, water your back yard. Do it at night so the neighbor's don't cop you out.

Since the 1980s we have had the world's largest solar power plant, Ivanpah, situated on a stretch of land larger than New York's Central Park. Out in the Mojave Desert, three hours from Los Angeles, rows of trough-shaped mirrors collect and concentrate the sun's heat and ultraviolet radiation to cook tubes of synthetic oil up to 750°. The hot oil is piped to a generating station to flash-boil water, making steam that drives a traditional power turbine. This Kramer Junction plant has been reliably providing about 350 megawatts of peak power to the L.A. grid, power for more than 150,000 homes, for almost twenty years (Nova PBS, 4/07).

Finally a second thermal trough, that is what they call a plant of this kind, opened in 2007 outside of Las Vegas, Nevada. Instead of oil, this plant uses salt to store and release the heat to provide 64 megawatts of power to the grid, enough for 32,000 homes. The fact that it is smaller, took so long to happen, and is owned by a Spanish company only slightly lessens the fact. A third plant, a photo voltaic generating grid built in 2007, supplies about a quarter of the energy to Nellis Air Force Base, also in Nevada. A fourth in California in 2008 built by Stirling uses a sun gathering dish with its own engine to produce up to 1,750 megawatts that drives pistons to produce enough electricity for over 800,000 homes.

Come on you other states! Do Nevada and California have the only view of the sun? Exxon might own most of the solar patents, but let's get cookin, solar cookin. And here comes California again! In November of 2014 the latest world's largest, Topaz, was opened generating 550 megawatts! Here comes the sun! (Actually, you coal-burning troglodytes, the sun has been coming every morning).

New York competition? Might not have those flexible California girls, but it does have flexible, thin-film solar modules on the roof of the Stillwell Avenue subway station. It's one of the world's largest thin-film, building-integrated installations. Sixty thousand square feet of panels! 210 kilowatts of power! Enough to meet two-thirds of the station's energy requirements. So even in the sunless east, a window to the sun opens.

If thin film is good, is thinner better? What about solar paint? Imagine generating electricity via the paint on your house or business. Nano-solar paint, now under development, works like a silicon solar panel but at a fraction of the cost. At its heart is a dark, sunlight-absorbing paint coated onto the surface of aluminized mylar, which conducts electricity. A protective clear layer of indium tin oxide that covers the paint also conducts electricity. When sunlight strikes the paint, electrons are knocked loose, reaching wires that channel electricity to the home. I hope, I hope, it is not toxic for the environment, because my next house might have solar paint! Quite a few companies have jumped into this development race. Imagine, a city painted with solar paint. I would run the city.

If I don't live that long, paint my tombstone to power a light at night. Or at least my urn. I was afraid of the dark as a child, and you know, as you age you lose logic, control, and adulthood. Thank god—or whoever figured out that death was good.

Green cemeteries! Where you bury your body (or someone else who can walk does it for you) without a coffin and without a tombstone, using only a natural marker (or take your GPS triangulator with you). That way you nourish the earth, and if you have not done well in your life, you can still leave the earth a little better in your death, and rest assured and in peace, the earth will still treat you egalitarianly in your reprocessing.

If we're speaking of graveyard, we must be nearing the end of four, color coded generations: We've watched my Dad step out of the golden harvest from his fathers

South Carolina farm into the Silver Shadow of Pandora's Shop, then I "educated up?" into a white-collar, bookish existence that began to understand, but was slow to act. And those three steps of farm, factory, and wired white-out have rocked our world. It still is shaking. It is breaking. And are we strong enough to begin the mending and pass it to the Green Hope of our children?

And Der, as we fade into the gray world of our making, we can still help this Greening Generation go greener; then maybe the epigenome will take, and our grandchildren will inherit the activated green gene. Research has confirmed that some life style can be passed down the epigenome to your offspring. Lamarck was not simply a pigmy forerunner of the giant Darwin, but a primary evolutionist who argued strongly for the position that environment influences heredity. I always thought his argument made logical sense, but until recently, there was no corroborating evidence.

Can we leave any blessings behind to our green generation? A Senegalese Ecologist tells them:

> In the end, we will conserve only what we love. We only love what we understand.
> We only understand what we are taught

> -Babia Dioum

So greening generation, teach your children well. Better than we taught you. And learn from them, quicker and deeper than we have learned from you. Since much of this transgenerational book has been contained in the compartment of Grand Civil Supreme, hurtling on civilization's road toward the *Bridge Out: Full Speed Ahead*, some lines from Crosby, Stills, and Nash seem appropriate:

You who are on the road must have a code
       that you can live by.
And so become yourself because the past
       is just a good bye.
Teach your children well, their fathers' hell...
Teach your parents well, their children's hell...
       ...and know they love you.

Go, grow, green gene, may you prosper and
multiply. The earth loves you and thanks you. The universe
loves you and blesses you. And I just love you. What more
on this greening earth could anyone ever want?

So in a green conclusion that you have long been
longing for, green does seem bursting out. Will it stay? Or
like the brief burst following the first earth day, will it blow
away with the wind? Let's not let this earth resurgence
stop! It is for the rest of our life, for the rest of our
children's life, for the rest of the life on earth. Let's codify
it in our wills, and in our wishes, and in our blessings to our
children. Let them be, oh let them be, let them be green!

the solution

Der: "Damn it! Another chapter? You didn't list this one in your table of contents, and it does not follow your pretty color code of gold, silver, white, and green. I am slamming this book shut. Now!"

Kirby: "Please don't. For three reasons: I was not intentionally *mis*leading you; you get more for your money; and staggeringly, stunningly important--this has the answer."

Der: "Answer to what? You're a megalomaniac if you think you can solve the world's pollution problems. And what color is this section anyhow?"

Kirby: "It's a clear, see-through color because it will let in a lot of light; and it answers the huge problem of Grand Civil Supreme, of that sooty siren Pandora, and tells us how we turn the massive inertia of culture, and save civilization."

Der: "I've had it. An invisible color that saves the world? You're a nut case. I give up on you."

Kirby: "Hold it there. I won't challenge *the nut case*, but I did call the last chapter *The Green Hope.* That's not giving up. Certainly you wouldn't want to give up on your children, would you?"

Der: "That's a low blow, nice try but I still won't waste another nano second of my neocortext on your verbal BS. Goodbye."

Kirby: "Der, don't go! Not now when I've got the solution! Don't jump ship, I mean car—you haven't had the train jumping experience I have had, and it hurts. And I love you. I love anyone who has gotten this far. Let me tell you why I have not told you this earlier.

While writing the book, I saw no hope. If, as my son said, everything in my house hurt our world—and he was right--by extension almost everything in our culture has hurt our world. Let me repeat that: *Almost everything in our culture hurts our world.* Despite the best efforts of individual heroes, we are well on our way to a poisonous death from our own chemical offal.

A year ago I wanted to unplug myself from the polluting grid and slink into the woods and curl up in a cave—or, if I had the guts, find a cliff to fly from. I was sinking without a solution into the quicksand of our culture. I could flail and struggle in vain, or just quit and luxuriate in our decadent energy and material policies. I saw no hope. That's why I wrote so rawly.

But eureka! Revelation! Insight! Apple falling! In writing the book I have found a way that we might transform our culture without destroying it. I know how to stop the huge hurtling mess of Grand Civil.

The solution is as conceptually simple as it is practically hard. However, had I inserted the solution into the middle of the book, I would have had to discard my ironic humorous tone and I would have deprived you of this rollicking read. Therefore, in my scriptoprudence and narcissism, I did not go back and soften the earlier harsh tenor, because I was having too much fun cursing at our idiocy--and besides, I thought the sharp tone might wake some sleepers. And I was trying to awake myself.

It's easy to criticize. Easy to ridiculize.

Now I'm going to do the hard part. Solve. Be constructive. Tell you how hard I need to kick my ass and in what direction. And since it's tough to kick one's own ass, I'll kick yours and you kick mine. I told you Der, I need your help to kick this ole world back into orbit.

We need a sea change, and since many of us live on land, we also need a land change, and since a few of us breathe, we need an air change--sounds like we need an earth change.

Wrong. We need a cultural change. The earth is fine, I lied implying it is out of orbit. It is we bipedal, asphalt, industrial, financial, greedy animals that need to change.

So, how to do that?

1) We might look for a savior to start a new religion. I asked my closest friend, who I thought was considering accepting the role at one time. To persuade him, I even offered to be one of his followers. That made up his mind. He declined saying: "Kirby, I'm not sure I want you for one of my disciples."

Existential cardiectomy.

Looks like the savior might not come.

2) A new mythology? A new story of who we are: I'll start the new myths. Heck, if the head holds I hope to write my grandchildren stories. I think I can, I think I can replace *The Little Engine That Could* and *Mike Mulligan's Steam Shovel* with *The H-Man, The H-Girl, The H-Mobile, The H-World. The H-Heaven*, and all the other heavenly Hs.

3) A new constitutional amendment? How about the 29th Amendment: *Life, Liberty, and Earth Friendly Actions.* Before I begin to seriously develop a book called The 29th, Amendment, of course you will want to know what happened to the 26th, 27th, and 28th. I figure it will take a while to roll our culture over to earth friendly, so we had better leave space for anti-flag burning, anti-gay marriage, and those other more gravid amendments that might arise like anti-constitution burning, anti-congressional laws

burning, and pro-sign burning for scurrilous signs like: Bridge Out: Full Speed Ahead.

Actually, there are usually hundreds of amendments to the constitution proposed in each Congress. The 109th Congress (05-06) proposed constitutional amendments such as: a balanced budget, reproductive rights of women, school prayer, presidential line item veto, and the right to filibuster.

There is a way to stop most of the madness. I tried and failed, but it is a lot easier for you now with social media. Back then, while Facebook was still in the colleges, I created a website called: *TheEarthAct.org*

I would like to call this idea profound like $e=mc^2$; but maybe I can just call it simple, simple to understand and hard to implement. Here it is: *be=ppc*.

A **B**eautiful **E**arth equals **P**eople **P**ressuring **C**ongress. Congress has the constitutional mandate *"to promote the general welfare."* The general welfare is our health. So Congress has the duty and the power to legislate clean air, water, and healthy land. We have the power to force them to do it. They need to place our nation on a non-polluting, renewable energy basis. And they will if we the voters, we the **P**eople, pressure **C**ongress. They will legislate pollution-free houses, pollution-free transportation, and an absolutely strict manufacturing of poisonous materials. This three-step plan will be explained shortly.

It's that simple—our part as the **P**eople is to support **C**ongress with our voices against the lobbyists. The vocal cords of the lobbyists are lubricated with money, and Citizens United has let the rich in to rule. But whose country is it? Let's roar louder than their money. And whose health is it? Let's roar still louder. And who are you going to vote for? Let the individual legislators keep their jobs ONLY if they vote as the constitution demands, as we the **P**eople demand.

This should be a slam dunk. We all want it--clean air, water, and land/food. But this simple formula took four years of frustration to enter my simple mind—remember that challenge from my son to show him a single thing in my house that had not hurt our world? Though I had co-authored a successful college book called *Thinking,* I could not think my way out of the vast weight of our civilization crushing down upon the biosphere of our planet. (Yipes! We're in that biosphere!) I was blinded by and trapped in the global warning dream of a house, car, and stuff. Whether I turned on the stove, hopped into the car, or even put on a pair of shoes, I was hurting our planet. Caged in our culture like an animal, I paced and thought.

The Earth Act is simple to understand and most can agree with it. Read it and see if you can agree with it.

> *I am a citizen of the United States. I am a member*
> *of the living community of the earth. I breathe*
> *earth's air, drink earth's water, and eat earth's*
> *food. I will try to lessen my harm to our earth, and*
> *to pass our earth forward, better and more*
> *beautiful.*

This *Earth Act* is a unifying statement that cuts across political, geographical, religious and ethical boundaries. I vetted it with red necks and green guys, scientists and humanists, accountants and artists, teachers and students, republicans and democrats, techs and farmers, doctors and nurses, and the clerks at the quickstops. These diverse people have signed the Earth Act.

More importantly, they represent a huge number of voters who would also sign the act as they became aware of it. And if this group stayed united, they would outweigh the lobbyists. Congress always yields to voters over lobbyists, or they will not have a job to continue to receive the campaign money and perks from the lobbyists.

You don't have to be perfect and give up your SUV, like one of my friends pleaded as a reason for not joining—

in fact, if this organization spreads, you can keep your SUV because it will become a non-polluting one. Yes, it is possible. Remember the H-car.

There are enough organizations and groups that if they gathered under only one umbrella of clean air, water, and land (food) congress would be pressured (and they would be happy to have the back-up pressure, because they too eat and breathe and drink) to pass something like the following. If you are in one of those groups, please start joining with others. Here are three, workable bills from congress that would change our country.

The Earth Housing Act: "In five years all new houses must be built to use 100% renewable, non-polluting energy." Since these houses are already being built, and since the buyers recoup their purchase price in energy savings and a higher resale value, the resistance to such an Act would be limited.

The effect would be huge, cutting about a third of our CO_2 emissions.

The Earth Auto Act: "In fifteen years all new autos must burn 100% renewable, non polluting energy."

That's it. Congress has the duty "to promote the general welfare," and clean air is clearly our welfare. They can legislate it. Today.

But they won't, until all of us demand it. For the opposition to *The Earth Auto Act* will be massive, driven by the oil industry. Those black slimers continue to sell us polluting oil at unheard of record profits, so why should they want us to burn hydrogen, which is as free and as plentiful as the ocean? When the petrocrats scream, you have enough information in this book to thrust up your index and little finger at them. At the same time slap your other index finger across those two. Try it! You have just formed an H for Hydrogen. Now in a fluid motion with both hands joined into that H, raise that H sharply upwards in a two-handed salute quite analogous to the upwards thrust of the European fist as the bicep is slapped. How vigorously you do so determines much of the meaning. Go ahead, try it. Good job. A few more times and it will feel natural.

The beauty of that H salute is that it can be thrust in perfectly polite society. That is your acceptable response to all the BS about the Hydrogen car being decades away. Remember François Isaac Rivaz. Remember 1807! Over 200 years ago! The very first internal combustion car was a Hydrogen Car. Remember other countries are using them now. Remember the sun and air and waves can generate Hydrogen--pollution free! Remember the FCX and HR7, fast, long ranged, and pollution free. And now Toyota has released the Mirai (strange name?).

So give them the H sign.

With those first two earth acts of buildings and transportation, we will solve about 65% of our pollution problems. It also solves most of the Global Warming problem. There. I said it. This is the strongest position I have yet seen to counter Global Warming. If the United States leads, other countries hopefully will follow. Why wouldn't they want to drive their economy on the energy in water released by the sun and the wind. The Oil Wars will cease, and you will breathe and sleep better.

Simple.

We know how to do it.

We just all get together and demand that Congress does it.

For our health, for our children's health, for the health of the earth.

And as an added beauty, doing those two pieces of legislation will barely impact the technological convenience of our life. It is too simple. It's good for the earth and us. It's free.

These two steps of *The Earth Housing Act* and *The Earth Auto Act* allow us to own our beautiful, American dream of a home and a car, without polluting!

The Earth Materials Act: Now, the more challenging congressional bill: "All materials must be taken from the earth with minimal impact to the earth, and used in manufacturing in ways that do not release any poisons into the air, water, or onto the land." This step gets harder, but also doable. It would stop almost all of the poisons that we now manufacture. Put simply—if it pollutes, you can't make it. Simple. Release no poisons into the air and water, or onto land. Follow the first Hippocratic Law of manufacturing: Thou shalt do no harm. Nada. Nothing. Zippo. Zero. Cipher. No, not even a little.

Strict? Yes. Pure? Yes. Healthy? Yes. Difficult? Yes. Possible? Yes. Worthwhile doing? Yes.

And if some "poison" like cadmium in your phone is absolutely needed, and our creative scientists could not develop a substitute, then the manufacturer would have to put a rebate on the product, buy it back, and re-process the poison. That cumbersome project would hasten their search for alternatives.

Imagine what would happen if our buildings and transportation and manufacturing quit polluting! A whole new High Clean Tech! In all forms. Quite possibly the fourth huge job surge in our country, following farms, factories, dotcoms, and now—High Clean Tech! We could again gain leadership in the world, for soon all countries, choking on coal and on our old manufacturing processes, would want to, would have to follow us.

So, you can take action now! I failed with The Earth Act. Few people ever left it, but it did not spread. At the time, the blog was the main online medium, and I failed to blog more than once a month: I did not offer membership opportunities and actions; when Facebook became popular, I did not set up a page, and failed to use the other social media. If you wish to laugh at the old-time marketing, I passed out business cards with the site's address. Okay, I'm old with cuneiform methods. But you are not!

I ask your help! Please! I'll beg, or write you a poem if you can take the idea and run with it on Facebook, Twitter, linkedin, Pinterest, googleplus, tumblr, instagram and anything else to make it go viral. I failed at my website, and it partially opens, but is defunct. But you can start something! I repeat--we all want it, we just have to band together, online, in a large enough group. Even the corporate leaders who also happen to like to breathe and don't like the look of China's air, want air, water, and food, and I think they would be willing to support the legislation if all companies were bound by law, for the playing field would be level, and their consciences would rest sweet at night. Also, that large group that has come together with your help, would be their buying consumers.

Your group, call it what you wish, would not be in competition with any other organization, green, grey, giant or small, because you would not have to demand fees, just donations to help you run it. In fact, CEOs of NGO green groups are encouraged to talk to each other and consider this or a similar organization as a collective, focusing force whereby you can bring all your power of numbers together to enact valued legislation.

A free grouping of Americans! Like America was. And will be. Like our air and water should be.

Start now. Share this statement. Send an e-mail to your friends and ask them to pass it forward to their friends to join together and start something. Let the word loose just short of spasm and spam to any associations, groups, co-workers, churches, all social media, even your old fashioned Christmas card list.

If you can get it going, you will then have the challenge to keep the activity up for the long haul. We have seen too many groups like Occupy flash and fade. This is for the long haul, the revolution of America's energy use.

For all who want a clean green earth, and a true blue

sky! Let me be redundant (something I have not done in this book) and re-explain the tremendous potential: the first two simple acts of Congress, building and transportation, remove most pollution. We know how to do it. The phased-in costs would be far less than our recent wars, and the change would produce an enormous American clean green energy industry bursting with profit, yes, profit and jobs!

It pays to be healthy and green, and to live in accordance with the laws of life that are larger than our Grand Civil Culture, which even now hurtles through the sign: *Bridge Out: Full Speed Ahead.*

One of the best ideas to achieve a similar goal, is from Lawrence Lester who has begun his May Day campaign to get big money out of elections and lobbying, and return congress to serving the people. A congress such elected and representative of the people, not just the money and corporations, would pass sane energy legislation.

As a long-odds solution, I wrote *Tis for Thee: that we pledge our lives*, first edition called: *America the Takeback.* I took a sabbatical and tried to sow the seeds on college campuses. The novel shows a way for youth to hold their idealism, which most of them start with, and not lose it and sell out as they rise in power. Hopefully it is working, and easily available on Amazon.

So Der, thanks for taking my myopic journey. It's not quite as lonely now. Together, you and I and many others can open that man-made mechanical fist that clutches us, and we can stop smashing our earth, smashing all life, and the smashing of you and me.

Loren Eiseley said such a book would work only if the author was "nakedly honest and did not pontificate."

I've got that half right.

author's afterword

I just can't quit. (Admit you don't want me to, either.) So let me tell you the three things you can do to turn Grand Civil away from the Bridge Out, and thus save the world.

1--Burn this book. But do it without getting any particulates into the air.

2--Pass this book to a friend. Please. And buy a bookshelf copy for yourself. And one for your dashboard. It is also in e-book form, easy to help pay it forward. I've just put it on Kindle for 99¢

3--Start an online organization such as TheEarthAct to gather the people to pressure congress.

4--Four? Okay, I said three. Cheating again by the numbers—Full Green Speed Ahead!

In hustling my previous book to change the world, I described myself as tilting at a windmill on the moon. In this book, Der, the windmill has left the moon and now sits there facing us, facing you. I am still tilting, slightly, but someone with far greater computer and communication and connection skills will have to do it. It's hard, but tiltable. Doable. You can brake Civil Supreme, dismount, and put our citizens feet on *terra firma amanda*: on firm earth that ought to be loved.

www.ingramcontent.com/pod-product-compliance
Lightning Source LLC
Chambersburg PA
CBHW060618290526
45793CB00001B/67